P9-CQN-396

Parenting Principles

From the Heart
of a Pediatrician

Parenting Principles

From the Heart of a Pediatrician

William T. Slonecker, M.D.

"Family is where it's at. Other than my relationship with God my highest value is family. I am grateful for this dynamic book. It is written by a man who knows what he is talking about and practices what he preaches. It would be wonderful if this book could find its way into the hands, the heads and the hearts of parents everywhere."

—**Dr. Adrian Rogers,** *Pastor of Bellevue Baptist Church in Memphis*

"Bill is on target in this comprehensive and practical guide to rearing Christian children in an ungodly world. The Biblical advice is aimed at the child's heart to provide information that parents need to hear."

—**Dr. Bill Bright,** *Founder and President of Campus Crusade for Christ International*

"Dr. Slonecker has developed a no-nonsense style of parenting born in the womb of experience. His years of practice as a pediatrician have allowed him to be not only doctor, but counselor, mentor, and a purveyor of common sense and wisdom. Dr. Slonecker's unique insight gives him credibility to speak to a culture in desperate need of his values."

—**Dave Ramsey,** *Author of four national best-sellers, including* **Financial Peace**

"Parenting is very personal stuff. Nothing ruffles feathers like giving advice on disciplining children. Yet confusion and uncertainty are rampant in many homes. Dr. Slonecker offers solid guidelines for parents. You may not agree with every suggestion, but *Parenting Principles* provides a healthy prescription of wisdom to all who take time to listen."

—**Steve Green,** *winner of six GMA Dove Awards and four Grammy nominations, with over three million albums sold*

"Janis and I trusted our most precious gifts, our children Kristin and Josh, to Dr. Slonecker's care. Over the years he has not only been our kids' "Doc," he has been our trusted friend and Christian brother. This book is filled with his insights and observations gained through years of hands-on experience with thousands of children. If Dr. Bill says it — I believe it!"

—**Larry Gatlin,** *Grammy Award winner, numerous #1 songs including "All the Gold in California"*

"Dr. Bill Slonecker is and has been a friend and encourager to our family for over 30 years. Dr. Bill was pediatrician to our daughter Michelle and our son Shawn. During those years, he was more than a doctor to our family, he has been a teacher of Godly Biblical principles. Those principles come from his 43 years of experience in the medical field and his lifetime of learning from these experiences. When Michelle became a mother, Dr. Bill was there to help as a pediatrician, but also as a friend who really cares. One more thing: the principles Dr. Bill taught us really work. Try them . . . you'll see."

Gary and Carol McSpadden

"I had the privilege of serving Dr. Bill Slonecker and his family for 17 years. I have read his book and find it to be faithful to the Scriptures and filled with interpretations and insights for parents. This book is of great value to anyone who wants to train their children in the ways of the Lord."

Dr. Millard Reed, *President of Trevecca Nazarene University*

"Retiring after 43 years of devoted pediatric practice did not remove Dr. William Slonecker's desire to promote common-sense, Scripture-based parenting skills. His book offers parents the perspectives of a unique qualified professional discussed as in the friendly atmosphere of a pediatrician's exam room. Read and adopt Dr. Bill's down-to-earth approach to promoting your child's positive behaviors."

H. Brian Leeper, M.D., *Pediatrician and former associate of Dr. William T. Slonecker*

"*Parenting Principles* clearly defines the acceptable boundaries of discipline. Dr. Slonecker has incorporated his personal experiences, as a well-known, well-respected pediatrician, with his Christian ethics to provide basic parental guidelines for discipline."

Ann Morgan, R.N., *Dr. Slonecker's nurse for 20 years*

Parenting Principles from the Heart of a Pediatrician
by William T. Slonecker, M.D.

© 2001 by Fredericksburg Publishing

ISBN 0-9673099-0-8
Library of Congress Catalog Card Number

First Edition, December 2001
2 3 4 5 7 7 8 9 10

www.parentingprinciples.org

Contents

I dedicate this book to my wife, Betty, whom I love, cherish, and adore. Without her constant efforts, I never would have been able to accomplish anything substantial in my life.

Honey, thank you and I love you.

—Bill

Chapter 1

First Things First

Train up a child in the way he should go,
and when he is old
he will not depart from it.

PROVERBS 22:6

M

oms, does this sound familiar?

We feel we are constantly saying "NO!"—"NO!"—"NO!"

How do I get them to eat their vegetables?

My two-year-old throws tantrums. He whines and cries when he doesn't get his way. He gets up at night and gets in our bed.

My child is screaming and yelling in public. It embarrasses me.

How about this?

Our children are constantly arguing and hitting each other.

DEFIANCE!!!

The baby runs the family!

Bedtime, bedtime, bedtime!

Ahh, the frustration—**welcome to the joy of parenting!** Can you relate? You probably can, considering these comments were all received from mothers in my office. They responded this way when asked what their biggest problem was in raising their children. One mother's response concerning her three-year-old was especially gripping, for you can sense her dilemma:

> *He is disobedient and has no respect. He thinks nothing of waking us at 5 a.m. regardless of how we discuss it with him. He has now begun to lie occasionally. He seems to deliberately disobey until the final straw when voices are raised and threats are made. We have major power struggles such as "Battle of the Bathroom!" Then, everyone comments on how obedient and good he is. It makes me wonder if I'm expecting too much. Seeing us upset makes him grin. I just know that he is thinking, "What power! I made Mom and Dad wave their arms and talk funny!" His latest thing is to wear winter clothes in ninety-degree heat. Then he will change his clothes three to four times a day, just for fun. However, when he is "caught in the act," merely clearing your throat sends him into tears!*

Can't you just see the gray hairs developing within the roots of this young mother's head? What should she do? How should she do it? Whom should she listen to?

Most parents would agree that children need to be disciplined in order to train them. But as you will see in the following comments from parents who were asked the greatest problem they have in disciplining, it is not as easy as it sounds.

Is spanking really an answer? Will it teach my child that hitting is a way to solve a problem?

How do I handle a situation where my child is just doing what babies do naturally—such as being curious—but it is something that he needs to learn not to do? I want him to be investigative, because that's how he learns.

We do not know what actions deserve discipline, we do not know how or what is the correct way to discipline, and we do not know when we should discipline. We need support!!!

So many questions. So many variances.

He would rather stay at grandmother's, usually because she'll hold him all the time, and she won't spank him when it is needed. She doesn't believe much in spanking, but she lets him hit her. We do NOT allow that.

This may be typical of my child's age, but it concerns me that I frequently feel forced to use "painful punishment" to get his attention. I want to be sure that I don't overuse it and thus damage its effectiveness.

I don't know the appropriate expectations for her age.

My husband is very inconsistent in his method of punishment and most of the time all he does is scream at our son. He threatens to spank him but hardly ever does. He won't punish him in any other way. Then he complains all the time because his son does not obey. But, of course, that is my fault!

If you are already a parent, you are probably now sighing and thinking, "I'm not alone." If you are expecting soon, I have probably just scared you to death. If you do not have children, I doubt that I have just encouraged your procreation!

Parents have been rearing children for so long that it would seem that all questions and problems related to discipline of children would be answered or solved by now. With all the advice, counsel, and leadership from grandparents, doctors, teachers, psychologists, and even TV talk-shows, it seems that the children today should grow up perfectly behaved, hardworking, and happy adults.

There is plenty of advice, but usually it's confusing and conflicting.

Somehow the job isn't quite that simple. There is plenty of advice, but usually it's confusing and conflicting. One says, "Be strict," and another says, "Let the child have his own way." Then, a newspaper or magazine article advocates a third course of action.

Many parents today are confused and lack confidence in their qualifications and ability to rear their youngsters successfully. Some try to raise a child like building a house or working a jigsaw puzzle. If a piece can't be found to the puzzle, parents then become anxious and discouraged. This then interferes with the proper discipline of their children.

So what is the answer? Where do we begin in this discussion of parenting? I have found that there are two elements of life from which we can draw reliable truth. One, of course, is the absolute unchanging truth found in the Word of God. The other is through years of experience where patterns have repeated themselves over and over. This book is a combination of both. I have sought to combine God's principles for parenting with nearly forty years of experience in applying these techniques. It is a combination of "Thus Saith the Lord" and "Been There, Done That."

The Word of God	Experience
"Thus Saith the Lord"	"Been There, Done That"

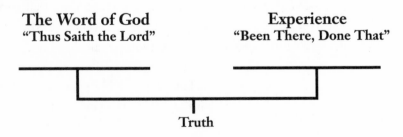

Truth

I believe the Bible is our guidebook for life. I also believe that its contents contain all of the answers we need to raise our children: God's way. Therefore, we will spend some time investigating it. Usually you will find that God lays out the principle. I will attempt to come behind the principle and support it with tried and proven ways to enforce it. In doing this I hope to build a philosophy for parenting packed with practical advice that will help you raise your children as God intended.

Now let's get something straight right at the beginning. Rearing a child is not a system; it is not an Einstein equation; it is not a Pythagorean theorem; it is not a 1-2-3 and your child will turn out fine. It is rather an art form; It's a Rembrandt, a Picasso, a masterpiece. If you are looking for a system, you will not find it here. If you are looking for something that will work, then you have turned to the right place. This book is about preparing the parents with the needed tools and proper techniques to enable them to paint to perfection the masterpiece God has intended their child to be.

What is Parenting?

There are many children these days with mothers and fathers, but few of them have parents. Just what is parenting?

Webster's Dictionary says that a parent is "one that begets or brings forth offspring." Pretty simple, isn't it? You become a parent when you have a child. Dr. James Dobson says, "Nature is somewhat careless about whom it allows to become moms and dads. Nature is not concerned with our happiness, only that we multiply. The qualifications are not very high to become parents. In fact, it is not necessary to know a single fact about a child in order to produce one."[1] Nonetheless, birthing a child puts you in the ranks of being a parent, but it doesn't make you a good one.

Parent-**ING** adds another dimension. *Webster's* says that parenting is "the **raising** of a child by its parents." So that little "**ING**" added to **parent** has changed this from a nine-month ordeal to an eighteen-year saga.

So what is our first step? What are we trying to accomplish with parenting? We must begin not with the tools, not even with the canvas, but with the finished masterpiece hung perfectly on your favorite wall, framed in all its splendor and grandeur. What is this masterpiece? It is a child who grows up and is found in the center of God's will for his or her life. That is my desire for every little boy and girl who is ever born into this world. This masterpiece is for all of God's children to find peace with the Master. That is our goal. That is our intention.

God gives us His definition and purpose in Proverbs 22:6.

Train up a child
in the way he should
go, and when he is old
he will not depart from it.

This is the promise from God in Scripture that every Christian parent hopes is true. It is the verse we claim when our children have us backed to the wall and we don't know where we have gone wrong. There are two points that need to be made here. The Proverbs are principles and not promises. Promises are guaranteed in Scripture, and this is no guarantee. If this principle is followed it will generally work most of the time. Remember that parenting is not a system that can be followed 1-2-3.

The second point is that a deeper understanding of the verse will show us that this verse is not an easy task. Too many are claiming this verse as a promise from God without ever doing their part.

WARNING: We are about to hear from "Thus Saith the Lord." It may get deep, but we must build a solid foundation.

Train Up A Child

God says to train the child. In studying this word in its original language, I have discovered three definitions that can be applied to the word "train."

• To "train" carries with it the idea of bringing a wild horse under control with a rope.

One pastor had this to say:

A boy is nature's answer to that false belief that there is no such thing as perpetual motion. A boy can swim like a fish, run like a deer, climb like a squirrel, balk like a mule, bellow like a bull, eat like a pig—all according to climatic conditions. He is a piece of skin stretched over an appetite, a noise, covered with smudges. He is like a tornado because he comes at the most unexpected times, hits the most unexpected places, a growing animal of superlative promise, to be fed, watered, and kept warm, a joy forever, a periodic nuisance, the problem of our times, the hope of a nation.[2]

The word "train" has in mind the taking of this bundle of energy and bringing it under control. This is the idea of discipline. We will spend many chapters dealing with effective means to implement proper techniques. By doing this, one can turn the problem of our times into the hope of a nation.

• **To "train" also can refer to developing a thirst or to stimulate an appetite.**

Back in the days of King Solomon, the author of Proverbs, the phrase "train up" was used in describing the action of a midwife. Once the child was born, the midwife would take her index finger and dip it into a bowl filled with the juice of crushed dates. She would then proceed to reach into the mouth of the baby and massage the gums and the palate in the infant's mouth. This would create the sensation of sucking. Furthermore, it would develop the thirst and appetite.

In order to train a child God's way, we must, as Christian parents, create within them a thirst for what is good and pleasing. Paul says in Philippians 4:8:

Whatever things are true, whatever things are noble, whatever things are just, whatever things are pure, whatever things are lovely, whatever things are of good report, if there is any virtue and if there is anything praiseworthy—meditate on these things.

Part of training children is to develop within them a thirst and hunger for righteousness. Not an easy task, but there are steps you can take to make it happen. Stay tuned—they're coming!

• **The third meaning for "train" is to dedicate or to consecrate.**

We are to dedicate our children to the Lord. I have grown up in the church and have watched hundreds of children being given back to God for His service and for His glory. That is a wonderful and Biblical thing to do. However, that is just the beginning of the process. Consecrating them to God is a promise to Him that you will do everything within your power to lead your children to a personal relationship with the Lord and Savior Jesus Christ.

So, in summary, let's review these three definitions:
1. Get Control
2. Give a Craving
3. Gratefully Consecrate

NOTE:
Some of you may be thinking about now, "Wow, this is a lot of religious stuff; I thought I was reading a book on parenting." Raising children is not a job you can leave to chance. I could write all kinds of current trends and unique approaches to parenting that may or may not work. However, we have chosen to go back to the basics. After all, God made us. He knows what will work. Why don't we give His way another chance?

Your Child's Bent

Back to our Proverb: "Train up a child **in the way he should go** . . . ." *In the way he should go*: Something is lost in the English translation. The Hebrew actually says, "Train a child in the way of him," in his own way, according to his own bent in life. Here, God is showing us that children vary. One of the reasons parenting is so tough is because children vary so much. This is why parenting is not a system. Every child is different. A godly parent is going to take the time to discover the child's bent in life, what makes him unique, and then train the child in that direction.

One thing worth noting: The child's bent will always be in complete agreement with the word of God. It is the parent's duty to distinguish between the child's depravity and the child's God-given design. For example, it is politically correct today to say that some children are born with heterosexual tendencies and some with homosexual tendencies. This is not scriptural. A child with homosexual feelings is a reflection of his depraved nature and not according to his own way, his own bent in life. The Bible teaches that God is against homosexuality, and a parent would do a great disservice to the child by training him in that manner. This is an issue I think more and more parents will have to deal with if our society continues in the same direction.

I believe God is trying to distinguish between training a child according to *the child's* way rather than according to *the parent's* way. So many of us try to raise our children the way we were raised. Each child is different. What worked on you will not necessarily work on your child. In fact, what works on one child in a family will not necessarily work on another child in the same family. Dr. James Dobson points out, "God has created us as unique individuals, capable of independent and rational thought that is not attributable to any source."[3] Train your child according to his own unique way. "Well," you might ask, "how do I know my child's unique way?" The answer to this is quite simple providing you do one thing: Spend time with your child. The more time you spend with him, the easier it will be for you to notice those things that jump out and cause your child to be so special.

One thing you can be certain of is that you are to train the child toward the way of the Lord. II Peter 3:9 says, "The Lord . . . is not willing that any should perish, but that all should come to repentance." You are to train your child in the fear and the admonition of the Lord. This is primary, despite his bent. The reason some parents no longer lead their children in the right direction is that they are not traveling that path themselves. Josh Billings said, "Train up a child in the way he should go—and walk there yourself once in a while."[4]

Don't be afraid to pass along a godly heritage to your child. Train them in the ways of God. Donald Grey Barnhouse told the following account:

An unbeliever once told Samuel Coleridge that he thought it was not right to bias the mind of a child with religious opinions. Coleridge showed him his garden, and when the man expostulated that it was covered with weeds, the poet answered that the difficulty was that the garden had not come to the age of discretion. "The weeds," he said, "have taken the liberty to grow, and I thought it unfair in me to prejudice the soil towards roses and strawberries." It is God who has said, "Train up a child in the way he should go; and when he is old he will not depart from it."[5]

In summary, train your child according to his own uniqueness. If you raise him exactly the way you were raised, there is no guarantee he will turn out like you; the fact is, he probably won't. Train him toward the Lord with all of his own idiosyncrasies.

When He Is Old

Solomon, the wisest man that ever lived, continued to say that if you properly train your child according to His way, **when he is old** he will not depart from it. Another nugget of truth that is lost in translation is the word for "old." When is your child "old"? This word in the Hebrew simply means "bearded one." A boy typically begins to grow a beard when he reaches adolescence. In centuries past, adolescence did not exist. Following puberty, one was an adult. There was no such thing as the teen-age years.

Your training should be almost completed when the child reaches adolescence. If he does not have it down by then, you have probably missed your opportunity.

He Will Not Depart from It

Here is where we come to the principle and not the promise. If you do all of these things, generally your child will follow the path best suited for him. There are exceptions. For those, we must pray and trust the Lord will bring them back on the right path.

The Goal

Here is the principle for Christian parenting given to you by God himself:

Train up, discipline,

develop a spiritual appetite for righteousness,

dedicate your child according to his own way,

so that when he reaches adolescence,

he will not depart from it.

This is God's definition of parenting. Learn it, memorize it, write it on the tablet of your heart and mind, put it into practice in your home. Only then can you claim it for your children.

Before tackling some of the tools to paint your masterpiece, I want to tell you about a place and a person that are extremely important in your child's life. While life's most influential place is the home, life's most influential person is Mom.

Life's Most Influential Place

Nothing outside of home can take the place of home. The school is an invaluable adjunct to the home, but it is a wretched substitute for it. The family relation is the most fundamental, the most important of all relations.

Theodore Roosevelt[6]

Parents today have an unbelievable challenge. The past twenty years the devil has masterminded a network of evil that has pervaded every influence on the home. The result has been a mass destruction of the institution that God designed for the main purpose of raising children.

We have seen the byproducts of this breakdown all through our society. Some statistics (1996) tell us that in one typical day in America:

> *The past twenty years the devil has masterminded a network of evil that has pervaded every influence on the home.*

3,288 children run away from home—1,096 never return. 4,896 children become victims of divorce.

2,784 teenagers get pregnant—1,128 have abortions.

1,104 teenagers attempt suicide—five are successful.

135,000 kids bring weapons to school. 3,610 teens are assaulted—80 are raped.

45% of teenagers are regular alcohol consumers. Six will die in alcohol-related accidents.[7]

Our government will spend millions of dollars this year trying to fix these problems. Everyone is trying to come up with a new way. We do not need a new way; we need to return to an old way. Build a happy, secure, godly home for your family!!! This is the best opportunity you have to keep your child from becoming a statistic. But how do you do it?

Six of the seven wise men of Greece were all asked what they felt constituted a happy home.

Solon said, "The house most happy is where the estate was got without injustice, kept without distrust, and spent without repentance." **Live honestly**

Bias said, "That house is happy where the master does freely and voluntarily at home what the law compels him to do abroad." **Live legally**

Thales said, "A happy house is where the master had most leisure and respite from business." **Live comfortably**

Cleobulus said, "That in which the master is more beloved than feared." **Live lovably**

Pittacus said, "That is most happy where superfluities are not required and necessaries are not wanting." **Live modestly**

Chilo added, "That house is most happy where the master rules as a monarch in his kingdom."[8] **Live powerfully**

There you have it: live honestly, legally, comfortably, lovably, modestly, and powerfully. Notice that these so-called "wise men" all relate the happiness of a home to the well-being of the master. I disagree. The happiness of the home is not determined by the status of the parent, but the well-being of the child. The home was designed for them. Adam did not need a home. The institution was created by God for Adam and Eve to nurture their "multiplications." Home was created for the children.

We need to remember that God formed the HOME before

> *The government, the school, and the church all have tried to pick up the shattered fragments of boys and girls who have been ripped apart because of the neglect of their parents to build a place called home.*

government, school, or the church. It is not the place of the government to raise your children. It is not the school's place to train them in the way they should go, nor does this responsibility fall on the church. All three of these institutions have tried to pick up the shattered fragments of boys and girls who have been ripped apart because of the neglect of their parents to build a place called home.

Someone has well said that many American homes nowadays seem to be on three shifts. Father is on the night shift, Mother is on the day shift, and the children shift for themselves.[9] If your deepest desire is to raise your children God's way, you must see the importance of the home environment. While you do not have the power from within yourself to build all godly homes in America, you do have the power to build one at your address. Go for it! Dedicate yourself to preparing a place for your child that will impact his life for all eternity.

When Oliver Wendell Holmes was once asked, "What is the most important factor in a man's success?" he answered, "He must choose the right parents."[10] The right parents build the right home.

Homemaking

In order to make a watch, you need a watchmaker. In order to build a home, you need a homemaker. God designed it this way, and He fashioned one particular member of the family to do it exceptionally well. Building a home is not easy. In my opinion, it is the highest calling. That is why God designated for Mom to be the primary homemaker. Wow, what a responsibility!

Now, I can hear some of you ladies beginning to question this idea. Some of you are thinking, "I'm just not cut out to be a mom." I saw a bumper sticker the other day that said, "My only domestic quality is that I live in a house."

You may have heard about the conversation between a husband and wife. The wife said to her husband, "The two things I cook best are meatloaf and apple pie." The husband quickly responded, "Which is this?"

Possibly your ideas of motherhood are negative. Maybe you have had the chance to see some of Art Linkletter's interviews with children. He asked one little boy, "How did God punish Eve?" The child answered, "He made her a housewife."

I can assure you that being a housewife is not a curse from God. Unfortunately, many people in today's society are trying to convince you otherwise. There is no greater calling. Let me give you some reasons why that is true.

• **Mom is the heart of the home.**

It has been well said, "The father is the head of the house; the mother is the heart of the house."[11] Moms hold it all together. They keep the emotional balance. My children grew up in a family of five, that is five very distinct and different personalities. Arguments were as often as meals; that is, there were at least three per day. While I looked for justice to be served, as men usually do, my wife wanted everybody to be happy. Her role was to build a happy home. I appealed on the rational level, with my head. My wife appealed on the emotional level, with her heart. I taught the children to think critically (which is important). My wife taught the children to think compassionately (which is more important).

A mother's heart is what transforms a house into a home. As we enter adulthood, we often contemplate the memories of home. I doubt we think of how the bricks were laid, or how the paint was chipped around the window seal, or where the stains were upon the carpet. But no matter what kind of home you were raised in, your thoughts are emotional. To me, memories of home bring forth feelings of comfort, security, love, and peace. For others who did not have the privilege of being raised in a godly home, they may have feelings rising within them of hatred, pain, bitterness, wrath, and injustice. Mothers, God has given you the role to make the difference in the memories of your children.

• **The child's fate is often determined by Mom.**

George Washington said, "The greatest teacher I ever had was my mother."[12] Napoleon Bonaparte said, "The future destiny of the child is always the work of the mother."[13] Mothers have a profound influence over their children.

It has been documented that the country of France had sixty-nine kings. All of them were despised by their countrymen except for three. It just so happens that history also records that those three were the only ones raised personally by their mothers. All of the others were raised by hired hands who were unable to give the loving care that only Mom can give.

Your child learns emotional stability from Mom. Mom transfers her heart feelings into the child in an almost supernatural way. Someone has well said, "Mothers write on the hearts of their children what the world's rough hand cannot erase."[14]

• **For Mom, it comes naturally.**

Girls and boys are different. My granddaughter, Mary Grace, has her "Baby Doll," which is her most prized possession. She cares for "Baby" and nurtures her as any mother would her newborn babe. "Baby" goes everywhere and anywhere with us and must be a part of bedtime, or there are BIG problems! This tenderness and care is built into her, just like her Mommy and Mimi. When Jack, my grandson, came along, we expected him to respect "Baby" and treat her as part of the family. Instead, we found he would rather take "Baby" by the neck, throw her across the room, and laugh heartily. This is all happening while Mary Grace falls all to pieces. Needless to say, girls and boys are different.

Watch the difference in how girls and boys carry their books at school. A girl will clutch them with both arms and hold them close to her heart, as if she were holding a child. A boy will carry them down by his side, if he carries them at all.[15]

These differences between boys and girls still exist when they become men and women. They can be seen in almost every area of life. For instance, when a man answers the phone he reaches for a pencil; a woman grabs a chair.[16]

No matter how much the dad loves the child, he is unable to transfer and communicate as effectively his emotions to that child. He is not built with the internal instincts of motherhood. Moms do not have to be trained to be moms; it comes naturally.

Ladies, please consider motherhood seriously. We mentioned earlier that Satan is attacking the home in every direction. One of those blows has come through a popular philosophy promoted by liberal feminists and the secular media that says that a homemaker is an inferior position in society. The devil knows that if he can keep mothers from nurturing and influencing the children at an early age, he will not have to do much to keep them in his camp when they grow old. Women, stand up and rise to the occasion. Your role as mom is crucial to the training of your child. No one can replace mom—no one!—not dad, not brother, not sister, not baby-sitter, not day care, not neighbor, not school, and certainly not TV. One of the greatest needs in our society today is godly mothers.

Where Do We Go from Here?

In order to train and discipline a child God's way, certain foundations have to be built. Much of the training of a child is found in the character of the parents. I felt the need to establish early in this book the importance of homes and godly mothers. Also, I wanted to give you the basic philosophy of the Bible for training children. Now that we have done that, where do we go from here in this process of training?

I want to give you a brief overview of the book in order to whet your appetite for what is ahead. In order to paint the masterpiece, certain tools must be used. The diagram you see below is basic and simple, yet illustrates parenting profoundly. I want to briefly go over each part of the process, and this, in some way, will give you a foretaste of what is ahead.

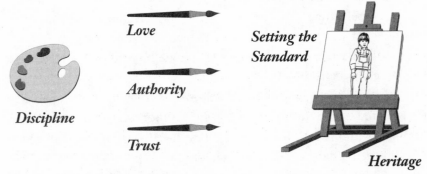

Setting the Standard—the Canvas

An important part of parenting is setting the rules and sticking to them. We all need boundaries in our life, but how should we go about setting them for our children? In this chapter we will illuminate God's principles for laying down the law. How does He do it, when does He do it, and for what reasons does He do it? We will answer all of these questions as well as help you apply God's parenting principles in setting standards in your own home.

Love—a Paintbrush

Next, we will address the need for unconditional love to saturate your home. We will look at the benefits of a mother's love and of a father's love as well as study some various techniques to aid you in loving your own child more.

Authority—a Paintbrush

Alongside love, authority is a necessary ingredient in the recipe of parenting. Everyone wants obedient children. Here we will paint the ideal, the goal to shoot for in accomplishing this. Many future discipline problems can be eliminated when proper use of authority is established.

Trust—a Paintbrush

After setting the standard, three elements are vitally important to build into your home in order to train your child in the way he should go. Those are love, authority, and trust, our three paintbrushes used to paint our masterpiece. We will examine this third element that often ends up being the missing link in proper parenting.

Discipline—the Paint

Anything you do to or for your child comes under the heading of discipline, or training. Love, authority, and trust are introduced to your child through discipline. That is why I have associated the paint that goes on the brushes with discipline. It comes in many colors and textures, and is full of both positive and negative techniques. The majority of the book has been devoted to this topic, as we will discuss the need for discipline and different types of rewards and punishments. We also will be answering the basic care questions for infants and the more complicated questions that come with dealing with older children.

Heritage—the Easel

Here we will conclude that the first priority of parenting is to instill within your child a Godly heritage. It is that heritage that will last from generation to generation. The easel is not good for only one portrait. It is that easel that will be used to paint scores of masterpieces generation after generation. Children are God's possessions that He has given us for a short time. You will see how God will fill the gap in any areas where you fail as a parent. He is sovereignly in control, and you will be thankful that He is.

Are you ready? It's hard to raise a family—especially in the morning. God has given you just a few years to mold their character. It has been said before: "Building boys is better than mending men."[17] If you have already started parenting, remember, "The largest room in the world is the room for improvement."[18] It is our desire that this book will applaud those things you are doing well and encourage you in those areas that are lacking. Always remember that what counts in the long run is neither the mountain top successes, nor the valleys of bungling mistakes, but the general average of training over the years. Unfortunately, as one grandparent said, "The trouble with being a parent is that by the time we're experienced, we're unemployed."[19]

Chapter 2

Setting the Standard

I n forty-three years of practice in the field of Pediatrics, I have had many letters from children come across my desk. One, in particular, that was rather disturbing came from a little girl six years of age. It was written to her mother, and entitled "The Monster."

> You're afraid of me!
> I throw things. I hit people.
> You pretend not to see.
> I talk back and you do nothing.
> You never tell me what I should or should not do—
> except in the most polite way.
> You are afraid of me! And I'm scared.
> Who knows what you might let me do?
> Please, please tell me when to stop.
> Don't be afraid of me.
> Sally

Children need boundaries! They need limits as to what they can and cannot do. A world without boundaries leads only to confusion and destruction. This is true even for adults. Can you imagine your world without limits and standards? Just think about it.

- *I got up at noon for my nine to five job.*
- *I skipped my bath because I didn't feel like getting wet.*
- *I looked into the mirror and smiled, noticing my rotting teeth that I never brushed.*
- *I drove ninety m.p.h. through my subdivision wiping out two bikes, a kid, and a dog.*
- *An old lady got in front of me, so I shot her.*
- *Traffic was backed up on the interstate, so I entered the expressway going in the opposite direction.*
- *I noticed on my way to work that it was a pretty day, so I decided to skip.*
- *I went to buy a convertible and couldn't afford it, so I bounced a check.*
- *I drove to the non-public beach to enjoy my day, where I saw a striking red flag blowing in the wind.*
- *As I was drowning, I wondered what that red flag meant.*

Imagine if there were no guidelines, no boundaries in your life—how confused and frustrated you would

Imagine if there were no guidelines, no boundaries in your life.

be as an adult. Imagine how confused and frustrated a child is without guidelines. This is why I compare this chapter to the canvas. It is our boundary in which we will paint our picture.

A life without limits ultimately leads to destruction. God fashioned us as creatures that need limits. Therefore, since it is our responsibility as parents to raise our children, we must set limits! But how do we do this? Let's take a few minutes and discover God's principles for setting the standard.

When we think of God's standard, our minds quickly turn to the Law, easily summarized as the Ten Commandments. At Mount Sinai, God laid down the Law to Moses. How should you lay down the law in your home? Let's see first how and why God gave His Law. This will help us in establishing our own rules for the home. We are going to look at three principles God's Law was designed to create. Consequently, these same three things should be considered in establishing the rules and regulations of your home.

#1. The Law Pronounces our Sin.

The Bible teaches us very clearly that the purpose of God's Law was to inform us that we had done wrong. Think about it: Without laws, is anything wrong? Of course not. Without the Law, man did not know when he was doing right and when he was doing wrong in the eyes of God. So, He gave us the Law to set those boundaries. Therefore, by establishing rules for your house, you are making known to your child right from wrong. That is principle number one.

#2. The Law Proclaims the Nature of God.

We have already said that the law reveals to us right and wrong according to the authority that made the law. Consequently, the authority is telling us through a law what he or she thinks is right or wrong. Hence, when we examine laws made by certain kings or presidents, we can learn a great deal about the nature of that leader. For instance, a president who legislates in favor of abortion, homosexual rights, and the legalization of drugs tells us an enormous amount of information about that president's character, morals, and values. On the other hand, legislation can show tremendous qualities in a leader. During the memorial service of President Abraham Lincoln, the Speaker of the House of Representatives, Schuyler Colfax, stated that the last law President Lincoln signed required the motto "In God We Trust" be inscribed on all of our national currency.[1]

Laws tell us so much about the nature of the authority that makes them. Here, you can tell by the law of Abraham Lincoln that he was a godly man. Therefore, the Law of God should tell us a lot about Him— and it does. God's Law reveals to us what His omniscience knows to be right. He drew the differentiating line between right and wrong with His holiness. Accordingly, His holiness keeps that line from moving from one generation to the next.

Another point worth noting is that God did not make a law that He personally was not willing and able to keep. The laws originated out of His character. His standards were defined by who He was. Consequently, He lived up to the standards that He set.

Bottom line, you can look at God's law and see what His morals and values are. Your rules need to be fashioned according to your morals and values. This way, you can live up to them. I would hope that your morals and values would be steeped in the Word of God and that you would strive to be blameless, pure, and right. This will set your child toward a life of godliness.

#3 The Law Pilots a Life of Obedience.

Obedience and respect for authority are greatly lacking in today's youth. God's law is designed to encourage a life of obedience. God understands the dangers of life better than anyone else. He has the best perspective. When a child of God breaks a law of God, he suffers the consequences of God. After repeating this painful process a few times, the child begins to realize a pattern. "If I do what God says,

When a child of God breaks a law of God, he suffers the consequences of God.

things work out for my good. If I do things my way, I get hurt. He must know something about life that I do not know. These rules are here to help me."

It works the same way with parenting. You have a better perspective than your child on the dangers of life. Your laws must come with penalties for breaking them. No matter how painful it is, penalties must be enforced. Without them, the laws are useless and encourage disobedience. With them, they develop within the child a trusting relationship with you as their authority. If they can trust and obey you as an authority, they are more apt to be obedient to authorities when they get out on their own.

Well, there you have it: God's method for setting standards. I realize that was a lot of theology, but now it is time to get practical. If you found the previous section somewhat difficult to comprehend, I would suggest that you reread it after you have finished this chapter. There are some important principles found there that I don't want you to miss.

Someone has well said, "It is by leaving the peace at home to chance, instead of pursuing it by system, that so many houses are unhappy."[2] Setting standards is a system. It is a system that I hope to explain well enough for you to incorporate into your home with confidence.

Who Makes the Rules?

I heard about one little boy who came to his mother and said, "Mom, I'm as tall as Goliath. I am nine feet tall." She asked somewhat puzzled, "What makes you say that?" He explained, "I made a little ruler of my own and measured myself with it, and I am just nine feet tall."[3] The Bible says in II Corinthians 10:12, "But they, measuring themselves by themselves, . . . are not wise."

Who makes the rules? Answer: the parents. I know this seems elementary to most parents, but you would be surprised how many couples get this confused. They let the children run the house and make the rules. The children decide when everyone gets out of bed, goes to sleep at night, and when and what they will eat for breakfast, lunch, and dinner. This is not right.

I remember one family in particular that I saw in my practice that let their six-year-old child make all the decisions. The child decided that he wanted to move to Memphis. Keep in mind the child was only six years old. The family sold their family-owned grocery store, packed up, and moved to Memphis. They were there about six months when the child had grown tired of Memphis and wanted to return to Nashville. The parents again submitted to the child's command and moved back to Nashville. The roles were reversed. This child was not capable of making a responsible decision, yet the parents, for some reason, felt pressure to comply. Parents are the authorities, not the children.

Children know their parents are the authority and will respond accordingly when the position is appropriately filled. It is not unusual for the growing child to imitate the parent as an authority. One little fellow was in hopes he could do this to get out of going to school. He called the school and the following conversation resulted:

Voice on phone: "Ernie has a cold and can't come to school."
School secretary: "Who is this?"
Voice on phone: "This is my dad."

Parents have the God-given responsibility to provide standards for the child. The child is simply not capable of knowing what is best, nor what is right. Remember the golden rule: Those with the gold, make the rules!

> *Remember the golden rule: Those with the gold, make the rules!*

When Do You Make the Rules?

Have you ever been traveling at night on a road that you have never been on before and you suddenly get the feeling that you are going in the wrong direction? You remember a fork in the road a while back that you passed without reading the signs. You frantically look for a marker, but none is found. You drive mile after mile in hopes of finding at least a service station, in order to ask your location. You slow down several times with the intent of turning around and going back, but your indecision drives you once again to check just over the next hill. Then suddenly you notice in the distance a sign. Your heart pounds as your car races for the marker. Ahhh, what a relief! You're heading in the right direction. Now you can continue your trip with confidence.

There is something about having markers that gives you confidence on your journey. A parent must inform the child of his or her boundaries through rules and regulations at a point that precedes their confusion. Give them markers in plenty of time to give them confidence on their journey.

> *A parent must inform the child of his or her boundaries through rules and regulations at a point that precedes their confusion.*

Let me give you an example of what I am trying to say. Hypothetically (and I am not saying that this age is what you ought to use), let's say you don't want your daughter to wear makeup until she is fourteen. You do not want to set this rule the day she comes home from school on her twelfth birthday and tells you all the girls at school are wearing makeup and asks you when she can start. If you tell her at that point that she has to wait two more years, her rooftop will blow. However, if you begin setting that rule when she is seven or eight and keep emphasizing that at fourteen she can start, then she will at least know well ahead of time when she will have her turn to wear makeup. Standards and rules need to be set in plenty of time so that the confusion and frustration in your child will be limited.

Sex education is another area where expectations and standards need to be set well in advance of your children's confronting the topic in another setting. This is not a one-time conversation. It is an ongoing dialogue you have with your children until the confusion is cleared up and the understanding is plain. You cannot afford to let someone else teach them this lesson. Place the marker well in advance and give them more and more understanding as you proceed. Again, you are building confidence to help them fully comprehend this wonderful gift of God that He reserved for marriage.

Many children in my practice failed to receive needed markers in their life. In the case of Jennifer, the events are still quite vivid. Jennifer had failed to receive needed markers in her life. While making my normal rounds in the hospital, I found a very belligerent, aggressive, and combatant twelve-year-old girl. Jennifer was so wild that the hospital staff was forced to use leather straps to control her. After speaking with her parents, I quickly realized the reason for her unruly behavior. The parents had never punished her, allowing her to always have her own way. There were no rules in their household.

As I approached Jennifer to examine her, she quickly turned her back to me. I walked to the other side of the bed, and again she immediately turned in the opposite direction. This process was repeated several times until my patience was exhausted. At this time I instructed the nurses to bring me a large pan of crushed ice. Once again, I approached Jennifer; she turned in the opposite direction. However, this time she was quite startled when a pan of ice came pouring over her back. The nurse refilled the pan. As I walked to the other side of the bed, she continued to turn away from me. Suddenly a dose of cold, breathtaking, attention-getting ice poured on the other side of her bed. This process continued several more times as she was surrounded with ice. Jennifer turned to me in frustration and said, "If you'll stop, I'll stop." The ice was removed from the bed. The next time I approached her bed, she again defiantly turned in the opposite direction. It was time for another lesson and the bed was coated thickly with ice. Jennifer looked up and said she was finished. I responded, "No, I am going to leave it there for a while this time." She had to learn who was in authority. After a few minutes, she pleaded for me to remove the ice. It was obvious that she was sincere by the increased inflection in her voice. She assured me that she had learned her lesson and was compliant the rest of the night.

The following morning Jennifer was ready to go home. Her mother and father realized the need to properly discipline Jennifer, but they didn't really know how and needed some practice. Therefore, I wrote a prescription to spank three times a day so they would get in practice. Spanking a twelve-year-old is not a typical practice that I recommend, but this was an exception to the rule.

As they were leaving the hospital, Jennifer was walking between her mother and father, and I was seated at the nurses' station. As Jennifer got even with me, she leaned back and stuck her tongue out at me. Her father observed this and swatted her quickly on her "seat of learning." I assured him that he had responded well, as he had taken control of the situation for the first time. These parents immediately changed the standard of discipline for their home. As a result, Jennifer made a drastic improvement in her attitude and behavior.

Jennifer was one who received direction late in life. Imagine how frustrated she was for so much of her life. I hope this emphasizes the importance for early childhood guidelines. This situation was a fortunate one. The parents had to be willing to completely change their interaction with their child. Most parents are not willing to do this. When should you set standards? Early, and keep the markers clearly visible in order to give your children confidence on their path.

What Rules Do You Make?

While I certainly cannot give you a list of rules for you to establish in your home, I can give you some guidelines as to the nature of what rules to make and what rules not to make. There are three general principles to remember in making rules.

Don't die on every mountain.

I asked a grandmother for some advice on parenting. She said, "Try and be patient." She went on, "I have found that as a grandparent, I am much more tolerant of letting children be children. I still use discipline, but I have found that many of the rules that I enforced on my children were simply for my own sake and not for theirs. I was so busy, I made unnecessary rules that were for no reason."

Not every action in the house needs a rule. Don't try to turn your children into robots. They will ultimately rebel against you as their authority. Major on the majors. Pick out the big stuff and concentrate on those. Choose your battles wisely, and don't die on every mountain.

Make sure the rules are in tune with the Word and not the World.

Donald Grey Barnhouse told the following story:

Several years ago, musicians noted that errand boys in a certain part of London all whistled out of tune as they went about their work. It was talked about and someone suggested that it was because the bells of Westminster were slightly out of tune. Something had gone wrong with the chimes and they were discordant. The boys did not know there was anything wrong with the [bell tolls], and quite unconsciously they had copied them.

So you will tend to copy the people you are most with; you will borrow your thoughts from the books you read and the programs you listen to, almost without knowing it. God has given us His Word, never out of tune, to set the standard for our song. Here is the absolute pitch of life and living. If we learn to sing by it, we shall easily detect the false in all of the music of the world.[4]

This is even more important in this day and age. Everything from TV talkshows to the information superhighway is making impressions upon our standards. Parents, make sure that all of your rules and standards line up with the Bible. It is not out of date. It is unchanging and true. It is your measuring stick between what is right and what is wrong.

> *The Bible is your measuring stick between what is right and what is wrong.*

Do what is best for your child.

Always keep the rules in accordance with what is best for the child. God's rules are for our well-being. He says in Deuteronomy 5:29, "Oh, that they had such a heart in them that they would fear Me and always keep all My commandments, **that it might be well with them** and with their children forever!" In forming your rules, make sure that your child will be blessed by following them.

There are three basic categories that all of your rules should fall under: **Rules of Caution, Rules of Conduct,** and **Rules of Character.** Let's examine each of these.

• Rules of Caution

I read an interesting illustration in the *Leadership Journal* by a man named Timothy Munyon. He writes:

While living in Florida, I had several friends who worked clean-ing rooms at a nationally known inn located directly on the white sands of the Gulf of Mexico. They spent their work breaks run-ning barefoot in the sand. The problem was the inn required all employees to wear shoes at all times while working.

I noticed the employees responded in one of two ways.

The majority thought the rule restricted their freedom. The rooms had shag carpeting, delightful to bare toes, and just a few steps away lay the beach. To them the rule to wear shoes was nothing more than employer harassment.

But a minority of the employees looked at the rule differently. Sometimes late night parties would produce small pieces of broken glass. Occasionally a stickpin would be found hidden in the deep shag piles. Some knew the pain of skinning bare toes on the steel bed frame while making a bed. This minority saw the rule as protection, not restriction.[5]

It is your duty as a parent to establish rules for your child's protec-tion. Your child often will think this is a kind of punishment. Explain well to him that you are doing it for his protection.

Now many parents go overboard with this. Make sure that you are protecting them, but don't overprotect. Let them be children. They are going to get hurt. It is part of growing up.

Let me give you an example of this. Maybe there is a dead tree limb in the back yard that is especially high. You see a great danger in the child's swinging on it because it could cause a major accident if it were to break. Setting a rule not to swing on that branch is fine; however, some par-ents take this too far. An example of over-

Make sure that you are protecting them, but don't overprotect.

protection would be for a parent to tell a child he cannot swing in a swing set because he may fall out and skin his knee. Let him play. Part of playing is getting hurt. I know they are your precious children, but let them learn that there are consequences to their actions.

Rules of caution are not just physical. In fact, more important to the child's well-being is the psychological protection. We taught our children a little song that I'm sure you are familiar with,

Oh, be careful little eyes what you see.
Oh, be careful little eyes what you see.
For the Father up above is looking down in love,
Oh, be careful little eyes what you see.

Your children are dependent upon you to guard their pure eyes from the defiled material of this world. Of utmost concern is the television. This activity needs to be limited and strictly monitored. This goes for cartoons as well. The world's demonic philosophies have injected their values into animation and increased violence in these programs that are unheard-of for young children. Your child may or may not understand the reasoning behind limiting these sorts of activities. It doesn't matter. They will thank you later.

Saint John Chrysostom, the archbishop of Constantinople and a great orator of the ancient church, had this to say about this matter:

When we see a servant bearing a lighted torch we forbid him to carry it into places where there is straw, hay, or such combustible matter, for fear when he least thinks of it a spark should fall and set fire to the whole house. Let us use the same precaution with our children, and not carry their eyes to places of frivolity and amusement. If vain and wicked persons dwell near, let us forbid our children to look upon them, or have any conversation or commerce with them; lest some spark falling into their souls should cause a general conflagration, and an irreparable damage.[6]

• **Rules of Conduct**

Not only do you need rules of caution in your home, but you also need to establish rules of conduct. Many of these rules will come in the form of training good manners. Teach them the importance of saying "Yes, Ma'am," "No, Ma'am," "Yes, Sir," "No, Sir," "Please," "Thank

You," "You're Welcome." These phrases go beyond common courtesy. In most children of today, these words are missing from their vocabulary. Perhaps this is related to the overriding disrespectful attitude toward authority that is found in this generation.

Conduct is more than words. It is how you act. You desire your child to be respectful, well-behaved, and polite. You want him to perform to the best of his ability and do his best in every situation. There is a standard that I think is a necessity in the home that encompasses all of these things and more. It is called EXCELLENCE. Begin now to set the standard to perform with excellence. Roff Zettersten says:

> *Let us, as parents, teach our kids to reach for the highest grades in the classroom and for first place on the athletic field. It's not important that they finish number one, only that they push themselves to the limits of the skills and wisdom God has granted them.*[7]

These rules are to encourage your child in the Biblical principle of Colossians 3:23: "And whatever you do, do it heartily as to the Lord and not to men." In his book *Lyrics*, Oscar Hammerstein II points out one reason why,

> *A year or so ago, on the cover of the New York* Herald Tribune *Sunday magazine, I saw a picture of the Statue of Liberty . . . taken from a helicopter, and it showed the top of the statue's head. I was amazed to see the detail there. The sculptor had done a painstaking job with the lady's coiffure, and yet he must have been pretty sure that the only eyes that would see this detail would be the uncritical eyes of sea gulls. He could not have dreamt that any man would ever fly over this head. He was artist enough, however, to finish off this part of the statue with as much care as he had devoted to her face and her arms and the torch and everything that people can see as they sail up the bay.*[8]

By setting high standards in this area, you are demonstrating to your children the importance of conduct and self-respect. It builds within them self-esteem to know that others are complimentary of their behavior. This will give them the confidence to do greater things in the future.

You will certainly have specific requirements for your child in this area, such as "Don't put your elbows on the table" and "Say thank you after receiving a gift." Yet, most of the time this category should be left as a high standard, an expectation. The appropriate punishment for the child when he fails to give his best is a disappointed face from the parents. The ultimate reward for the child when he does his best but still doesn't finish on top is a parent so thrilled that one would think the child had just jumped over the moon.

• Rules of Character

"Manners carry the world for the moment; character for all times."[9] Many chapters of this book will deal with building character in your child, but it starts with setting standards. Sir Joshua Reynolds said, "Excellence is never granted to man, but as the reward of labor."[10] Work builds character. There is nothing wrong with giving your child a little work to do. Chores are good for him.

You may be wondering, "But I don't know what responsibilities are appropriate for my child's age." The following may be helpful.

Three-Year-Olds
- Get dressed
- Brush hair (girls may need help)
- Brush teeth
- Help in making bed
- Clear dishes from table (you might want to try plastic to begin with)
- Empty wastebaskets
- Put clothes and toys in proper places
- Put dirty clothes in the hamper

Five-Year-Olds
- Set table for meals
- Help clean bathroom
- Help clean and straighten drawers and closets
- Care for pets (feeding and walking)
- Dust furniture
- Help put groceries away
- Answer phone calls
- Load and unload dishwasher

Seven-Year-Olds
- Empty garbage
- Sweep walks and floors
- Help with kitchen cleanup
- Prepare school lunches
- Clean out car
- Practice music lessons
- Study
- Wash and dry dishes
- Help with care of smaller children
- Participate in organized sports
- Help with meal preparation

Eight-Year-Olds
- Clean bathroom
- Clean floor in small areas
- Do minor yard work and gardening
- Organize coupons for groceries
- Shampoo and shower without help
- Help with laundry—folding clothes
- Vacuum own room

Older Children

- Baby-sit
- Wash windows
- Paint with guidance
- Mow lawn
- Clean refrigerator
- Prepare meals
- Do yardwork
- Iron clothes
- Wash car

Your child needs to be given responsibility. This shows him that you are counting on him, and that he can be trusted. Don't expect your child to know right off the bat how to make the bed correctly. It takes practice. You will often be tempted to do it for him, but don't. Let him learn. Thank him and encourage him, especially when you see improvement.

Character, however, is more than just building a work ethic. Set standards to build integrity. Do not lie, do not steal, do not cheat. The best advice I can give here is to incorporate the Ten Commandments into the standards of your home. "There are over 35 million laws on our books in the United States and not one single improvement on the Ten Commandments."[11] The Ten

> *"There are over 35 million laws on our books in the United States and not one single improvement on the Ten Commandments."*

Commandments were designed to be taught in the home. Deuteronomy 6:7 says, "You shall teach [the Ten Commandments] diligently to your children, and shall talk of them when you sit in your house, when you walk by the way, when you lie down, and when you rise up." What better standard could be set in your home to build character into your child?

Okay, do you have it? There are three principles and three categories. The three principles are: Don't die on every mountain, Make sure the rules are in tune with the Word and not the World, and Do what is best for the child. The three categories are: Rules of Caution, Rules of Conduct, and Rules of Character. If you can pattern your regulations according to these suggestions, you will be well on your way to establishing the standards of a solid home.

What Rules *Not* to Make

We have already mentioned some of these. For instance, we discussed the importance of protecting your child, but the danger of **overprotecting**. You don't want to stifle your child's curiosity and sense of adventure.

Another common mistake that parents make in establishing rules is **not having a good reason for their demands.** An example of this is when you try to get your child to drink his milk.

"Tommy, drink your milk."

"I don't want to."

"I said drink your milk!"

"Why?"

"Because I said so."

Sound familiar? The infamous "Just Because I Said So" reverberates in the consciousness of all born of woman. Now, who is going to win in this situation—you or the child? "Just because I said so" should be removed from the parent's vocabulary. We must have a good reason for our demands on children. If you are unable to explain the reason in their own vocabulary, then you probably don't understand it well enough yourself for it to be a rule.

> *"Just because I said so" should be removed from the parent's vocabulary.*

A command with improper explanation may lead to a confusing situation. I heard of one child who asked his father one day after school, "If we go to school to learn how to better communicate with one another, then why do the teachers keep telling us not to talk?"

We often will bark an unexplained command at our child in order to control our own sanity. We may not be in the mood to answer. The old adage, "Children should be seen and not heard," can backfire. One little boy at the dinner table asked his father, "Are bugs good to eat?" His father replied, "Let's not talk about it now." After dinner the father came to his child and asked, "Now, son what did you want to ask me?" "Oh, nothing. There was a bug in your soup, but now it's gone."

As a child grows, so does his responsibility. Chores become more meaningful and significant. They are also more demanding. Make sure that you increase responsibility gradually. **Break at the natural breaks.** When they have mastered one thing, give them something just a little harder. Don't dump too much on them. I heard of one family where the parents required the children to buy their own groceries. They literally had to use their own allowance money to eat. There was a separate place in the pantry for their food, and they could eat only from that shelf. Children should not be faced with the pressures of providing for their next meal. These parents tried to break at an unnatural break.

Standards are Standard, Even for Mom and Dad

Parents, you have a standard to live up to in the home as well. Proverbs 20:7 says, "The righteous man walks in his integrity, his children are blessed after him." It has been said that a congregation cannot spiritually climb above the spiritual level of their pastor. I would like to apply this to the home. You as the parent cannot lift your children to a higher level than that on which you live yourself. You must faithfully live the principles that you are demanding from your children. If you tell them not to steal, don't steal yourself. If you tell them not to lie, don't you lie. If you tell them to keep a clean room, you had better make sure yours is spotless. Ask yourself this question, **"Can your children see in you everything that you want to be in them?"**

> *Can your children see in you everything that you want to be in them?*

A boy came home from school and showed his father his report card. The father said, "Not so good. Do you know that at your age George Washington was already a surveyor?" The son responded, "Do you know that at your age he was already president?" **Can your children see in you everything that you want to be in them?**

In John Taylor's *In Perilous Ways*, I read of the following true account:

> *An Indian catechist at the end of the last century was dismissed from the church for some misdemeanor. Burdened with shame, knowing he would never again dare to preach, the man left the area and went to some far-off, non-Christian area, where he settled down as a stranger and made his living as a potter. The church never heard of him again, and he died there.*
>
> *Later it was decided to send a team of evangelists to the distant area. They rented a house and started to tell the stories of Christ. They were amazed when the crowd of villagers responded eagerly, exclaiming, "We know the man you are talking about; he lived here for years." "Oh, no," said the preacher, "you don't understand. We are talking about Jesus Christ." "Well," answered the people, "he never told us his name. But the man you've described was our potter without a doubt."[12]*

These savages saw Christ in the potter. **Can your children see in you everything that you want to be in them?**

How Do You Make the Rules?

A child has the right to know what his parents want him to do and not to do. The standards must be understood by the child. It is not necessary for a child to agree with a standard—just as long as he understands it. You want your child to be able to answer correctly when you say, "Now, what did I say?" or "What does that mean?" In order to get this message across to your child, it takes some creativity and know-how. Here are some suggestions:

• **Get the child's attention.**

Before setting the rule, make sure to get the child's attention. Don't try to make rules while the child is playing Nintendo. Make sure to get eye to eye with the child and eliminate interruptions and distractions if possible.

• **Show your child you respect his feelings.**

Children don't like to be bossed around any more than parents do.

• **Say "Yes" before saying "No."**

You don't want to find yourself constantly telling your child "NO!" When he is interested in something that is a no-no, try to divert his attention with something else. Give him an alternative, a substitute—something to which you can say, "Yes." This will keep the atmosphere positive and not negative.

For instance, you may have a little boy who likes to make noise. He may have a stick and enjoy hitting it on your new coffee table. Of course this is a no-no. Instead of saying "No," you may want to go get some pots and pans out. Show your child that this will make even more noise. He will enjoy banging on these all the more. You have achieved two things with this solution. You have provided your child with a device that will intensify his enjoyment, namely, louder noise, and you have solved your troubles by protecting your furniture.

• **Give your child hope.**

Try as best you can to build within your standards hope for your child if he obeys. One very popular way to do this is with an allowance.

Allowances can be very good or they can be very bad. The difference lies in whether or not the child earns it. Allowances are positive when the child understands what he is to do, he does it, and then he receives compensation for his obedience. Children like money, but then again adults aren't allergic to it either. He will work hard to accomplish his chores and other work knowing that Friday is payday. However, if the child does not meet his obligations, the pay should be docked. Don't give your child an allowance just for being your child. If he earns it, he will appreciate it more and it should provide you with a better-behaved child with a more responsible future.

• **Give your child a role in setting rules.**

When children participate in making rules, they tend to follow them. Of course, this is almost impossible when they are really young; however, as they grow you can begin experimenting with this. Here, the creative juices must begin to flow. Let me give you a couple of suggestions that I have known parents to try.

First, the child chooses the punishment for the crime. After you as the parent have discussed with your child the reason and purpose of the rule, let him decide what punishment he should get if he breaks the rule. The probability of his keeping it will be much higher if he knows what the result of his offense will be, especially if he has set it. Make sure that the penalty fits the crime. Sometimes the child will be too lenient; and sometimes he will be too severe.

Another method you may want to experiment with is called the penny method. Start each week off with a jar of pennies, let's say fifty. Have a chart that indicates how much money will be deducted for each offense. For instance, failure to make bed, -5¢; failure to pick up toys when asked, -3¢; or talking back, -6¢. Any money that is left at the end of the week will go into his savings account. This way, the child sees that his choice to disobey will subtract from his rewards. He is in control of his destiny. It is the first stage of giving him some independence.

These are just some examples. Be creative. Be unique. Find out what works best with your child. The important thing is this: Make sure that your child understands the standard. Remember, it doesn't matter that he agrees with it, only that he comprehends it.

What are the *Contents* of the Rules?

The standards should normally include a **warning of the penalty for disobedience**. This penalty should be lovingly, but consistently, administered when disobedience occurs. The standards must not exceed the child's mental and physical abilities. It's only when a child comprehends a standard and has the ability to comply, that he then become fully accountable for his performance. It is very important that both parents agree on the standards and are consistent in enforcing them.

Don't let your child try to talk you out of the punishment in the midst of battle. If you give a child an inch, he'll think he's a ruler. Penelope Leach says,

> *Your child can have her say, put forward her point of view, and attempt to persuade you from your position to hers—but not in the heat of the moment. Tonight she sticks to agreed policy; tomorrow morning discussion may reopen.*[13]

Not only should the rules contain punishments for disobedience, but they should also contain **rewards for obedience**. It doesn't matter whether you are a nine-month-old, a nine-year-old, or a ninety-year-old; we all learn better through rewards than through punishments. The best rewards are not always in the form of gifts, especially not things that are harmful to them such as candy. Often a child is more thrilled with words of affirmation, or a big hug, or spending time with them, than they are with something you give them. After all, my incentive to live for the Lord here on Earth is not that I might receive a crown when I get to Heaven, but that I will hear from His lips, "Well done, my good and faithful servant." Applaud your children in their valiant efforts to be obedient.

How Do You *Enforce* the Rules?

Do you find yourself repeatedly bellowing the commands, "No!" "Stop it!" "I said NOW!" If you do, you can bet the farm that they are not taking what you say very seriously. If you are going to go to the trouble of setting standards, be sure to enforce them. Standards are to promote consistency. Your child needs to learn that he will reap what he sows. If you are not consistent, how can you expect him to be? Make sure that you and your spouse are in agreement.

The Bible says that the devil is more crafty and cunning than all of God's creations. That statement was made before God had seen children. They are smart little critters. They will sense quickly if there is any division between Mom's and Dad's authority. Dad says "yes," and Mom says "no." Don't allow this to occur between you and your spouse. You need to stop this in its early stages.

Most children favor parents who have standards and guidelines for them to follow. There is a common desire among children for some clear limits within which to operate—for some boundaries to push against or some rules to go by. Your child will naturally try to push against those boundaries. However, if you bend as your child pushes, he never can be sure that he has reached the limit. Robert C. Dodds says, "The goal in marriage is not to think alike, but to think together."[14] You and your mate must think together and draw one line where both of you agree to stand. Thus, when your child pushes, the line won't move.

Remember what God did with the Law. He drew the line between right and wrong and held it with His holiness. Salvation was not God moving the line. When we trusted in Christ, He did not shift the Law to now include us as sinners. The Law stayed firm, and its penalty was firm. We are saved through Jesus because He fulfilled the Law and credits us also as fulfilling the Law, because we trust in Him. The point is, the Law did not move. God stayed firm. You must model that to your children. When they push, demonstrate to them that the line doesn't move.

To Summarize

I want to take just a minute to take what we have just discussed and try to put it together with God's principles for setting standards.

1. The Law pronounces our sin. By having rules, your child will learn how difficult it is to be obedient and how natural it is for him to be disobedient. The Law shows his sinfulness.

2. The Law proclaims the nature of God. God's rules are established by what he knows to be right and wrong and governed by what is best for you as His child. The rules of your household should be derived out of your own beliefs. That way you can be consistent in enforcing them as well as living up to them yourself. Also God, through His rules, is showing you who He is and who He wants you to be. Can your children see in you everything you want to be in them?

3. The Law pilots a life of obedience. By setting standards in the home, your child will learn that obedience to authority produces positive results. This will be an invaluable lesson when one day he allows God to be his authority.

What's Next?

In Bob Mumford's *Take Another Look at Guidance*, an illustration is found that will help us in preparation for the next three chapters.

A certain harbor in Italy can be reached only by sailing up a narrow channel between dangerous rocks and shoals. Over the years, many ships have been wrecked, and navigation is hazardous.

To guide the ships safely into port, three lights have been mounted on three huge poles in the harbor. When the three lights are perfectly lined up and seen as one, the ship can safely proceed up the narrow channel. If the pilot sees two or three lights, he knows he's off course and in danger.[15]

There are three beacons to guide us into the proper training of our children. Any one of these three in excess, throws the ship off course. They must be perfectly balanced. The harbor lights for rearing your children are love, authority, and trust. They are our paintbrushes we will use to paint our masterpiece.

Chapter 3

Love Never Fails

*Love . . . bears all things, believes all things,
hopes all things, endures all things.
Love never fails.*

1 CORINTHIANS 13:7-8A

uess what happens to 3,502 fifth graders in America every day? They fall in love.[1] Just what is love? I am convinced it is one of the most misunderstood words in our vocabulary.

In the movie, *Arthur*, Dudley Moore plays a spoiled rich man who has never had to work a day in his life. Now while I don't agree with this philosophy, Arthur's worldview is to eat, drink, and be merry. And he does just that, at least in the movie. Arthur meets a young lady and thinks he has fallen in love, but he is not quite sure what that means. He asks a total stranger, "How can you tell if you are in love? Does it make you feel funny? Does it make you whistle all the time?" This stranger, who couldn't care less about Arthur's newfound flood of emotion, tells him, "You could be in love; then again, you could be getting sick."[2]

Love: What is it? I have found something in the Bible that proves that we do not have a proper understanding of love. In I Corinthians 13:8, the Bible distinctly says, "LOVE NEVER FAILS." When the Bible says love NEVER fails, it means it will never, no, not ever, there never was a time when it did, and there never will be a time when it will, FAIL. Now, here is our dilemma. In our society, marriage is the climax of love. Yet, many marriages end in divorce. By our definition of love, it fails. So something is wrong with our definition.

I was pondering this when my attention focused on the relationship of a mother to her son. Now that was love that never failed. I went back to I Corinthians 13 and read some of the preceding verses as I thought about this special relationship between a parent and a child:

> *Love suffers long and is kind; love does not envy; love does not parade itself, is not puffed up; does not behave rudely, does not seek its own, is not provoked, thinks no evil; does not rejoice in iniquity, but rejoices in the truth; bears all things, believes all things, hopes all things, endures all things. Love never fails.*
>
> *I Corinthians 13:4-8a*

When couples read this passage as they are preparing for marriage, they think, "Wow, that's tough." But when a mother reads this, looking into her child's face, she thinks, "Wow, how easy." It comes naturally for her. It has been well said, it is not until you have children that you know what unconditional love is all about.

Grandchildren take uncon-
ditional love to a new level. My
grandson, John William (Jack for
short), shares my birthday as well
as my name. He has been my
"buddy" from the beginning, and

*Love is a commitment that
endures all, believes all, and
demands all.*

we have had a special bond. Jack was born with severe reflux and had
this through his entire first year. Lots of unconditional love is needed to
deal with the projectile fluid of curdled milk and strained baby carrots
and peas oozing down your back. If this had been a patient, I would have
had to quickly find a facility for me to use, but this was my pal; I love
him; and it never bothered me. Unconditional love covers a multitude
of unpleasantries.

So as we begin the study of how to love your children, we do not
want to think of love as something you can fall into or something you
can fall out of like other emotional roller coasters. Love is a commitment that endures all, believes all, and demands all.

A chicken and a pig were walking down the street together when
they noticed a billboard. It read, "Ham and eggs breakfast, $3.99." The
pig looked at the chicken and remarked, "For you that is all in a day's
work, but for me, it demands total commitment." Love is a total commitment. It demands your all.

A Mother's Love

There is nothing quite like the love a mother has for her child.
Washington Irving described it this way:

> *There is an enduring tenderness in the love of a mother to a son
> that transcends all other affections of the heart! It is neither to
> be chilled by selfishness, nor daunted by danger, nor weakened by
> worthlessness, nor stifled by ingratitude. She will sacrifice every
> comfort to his convenience; she will surrender every pleasure to
> his enjoyment; she will glory in his fame and exult in his prosper-
> ity. And if misfortune overtake him, he will be the dearer to her
> because of the misfortune; and if disgrace settle upon his name,
> she will still love and cherish him in spite of his disgrace; and if*

all the world beside cast him off she will be all the world to him.[3]

One way that you can see a mother's love is in the way she talks about her children. One father said to another, "Has your son's college education proved of any value?" "Yes indeed," said the other one. "It cured his mother of bragging about him!"

One young mother was desperate to tell a friend more about her child. She said, "He's eating solids now—keys, bits of paper, pencils . . .."[4]

Mothers love to talk about their children. The Bible says in Matthew 12:34, "For out of the abundance of the heart the mouth speaks." A mother's heart is so full of love for her children that she can't stop telling you about them. That is love.

Victor Hugo described maternal love this way: "A miraculous substance which God multiplies as He divides it."[5] And just what is the result of a mother's love for her child? Listen to these great leaders of history describe the impact their mothers had on them,

"All that I am my mother made me."—John Quincy Adams
"All that I am or hope to be, I owe to my angel mother."
— Abraham Lincoln
"All that I have ever accomplished in life, I owe to my mother."
— Dwight L. Moody
"Let France have good mothers, and she will have good sons."
— Napoleon

Julia Ward Howe, when ninety-one years of age, said, "We talk of forty horse-power. If we had forty mother-power it would be the most wonderful force in the

Home is where mother is.

world."[6] Jacqueline Kennedy said shortly after she entered the White House in 1960, "My major effort must be devoted to my children. If Caroline and John turn out badly, nothing I could do in the public eye would have any meaning."[7]

Who can put a value on the love of a mother? Here you have some of the most famous people of history describing to you the influence of a mother's love. Perhaps, the greatest tribute ever to a mom came from a little girl who was asked where her home was. Her reply, "Where mother is."[8]

A Father's Love

The father's love for his child is not often thought of from the same standpoint as the mother's. While the mother's is one of empathy and emotion, the father's is one of provision and protection.

The following true story is one that demonstrates the driving nature of a father's love:

> *While the mother's love is one of empathy and emotion, the father's love is one of provision and protection.*

A steamer was wrecked on Lake Pontchartrain, on which were a father, mother, and their six children. The father was a stalwart man and good swimmer, and resolved to get them all safely to land or perish in the attempt. He told his children not to be afraid, that he would come for them. He then jumped overboard, and his wife after him. Taking her by the hair, he drew her along through the breakers, and landed her safely on shore. Then he plunged into the mad waves, and went back to the ship for his children. One by one he brought them to the shore. Only one remained upon the vessel. The devoted father had not strength to stand up when the last was brought in. Friends expostulated with him against the further exposure of his valuable life. He said, "Jimmy's aboard, and I promised to come for him." Then he floated back to the ship, and just as it was about to go down, he called to Jimmy to jump into the water. He had strength only to seize his boy, fold his arms about him, and press him to his bosom, and, thus enfolded, they sank together, to rise no more. Such is the love of a father.[9]

A father's love is often shown by the protection of and provision for his family. In this case, the father spent his own life trying to save their lives. While this story has an unhappy ending, don't miss the unconditional love shown by the father. The industrial capitalistic mindset of today's generation of fathers has caused an apathetic spirit toward their children. Love demands all. Are you willing to lay down your life for your kids? That is the love required. That is the love demanded.

It is natural and right for a father to show his child love not only by providing and protecting, but also by hugging and kissing. The stereotypes that say "Men don't do that" have raised a generation of kids who do not feel loved by their fathers. I remind you of what the Bible says about the father who had longed to see his prodigal son return. Luke 15:20 describes what the father did when he saw his son approaching in the distance, "But when he was still a great way off, his father saw him and had compassion, and ran and fell on his neck and kissed him." There is nothing wrong with a father showing physical affection to his children. In fact, there is everything right about it.

> *The industrial capitalistic mindset of today's generation of fathers has caused an apathetic spirit toward their children.*

God's Love

God's very nature is defined by love. I John 4:8b says, "God is love." Not only is God love, but He has demonstrated His love. The Bible says in Romans 5:8, "God demonstrates His own love toward us in that while we were still sinners, Christ died for us." The Bible says, "For God so loved the world that He gave His only begotten Son, that whosoever believes in Him should not perish but have everlasting life." For God SO loved the world. SO: There is a lot of depth in that little word *SO*. He loved us SO MUCH that He gave His Son—His Son. Can you imagine how much you would have to love in order to give up your son to be mocked and killed? What an incredible love!

God loves us, His children. He paid the ultimate price to redeem us. He gave His son to die for us. Jesus died in our place. This is the example that He has set out for us as parents. Max Lucado, one of my favorite authors, says in his book *And the Angels Were Silent*:

No price is too high for a parent to pay to redeem his child. No energy is too great, no effort too demanding. A parent will go to any length to find his or her own.[10]

Notice that God demonstrated His love when we were sinners. We were guilty before God. He did not show us love just when we did well. It was unconditional. We were sinners, and He hated sin. It is this unconditional love that is demanded. Your love for your child must be unconditional. There is nothing children can do to you to cause you to quit loving them. Your child may experience some heated

> *"Love demands all, and has the right to do it."*

moments of rebellion. You must continue to love him. Always, always, always, leave the door open for the prodigal son. That door swings on the hinges of unconditional love. Beethoven summed it up well: "Love demands all, and has the right to do it."[11]

Is Love Necessary?

The following story appeared in the magazine *Plus: The Magazine of Positive Thinking*, by Fred Bauer.

It was a well-run hospital with a friendly and dedicated staff. The health care was the finest available anywhere. That's why it was such a shock when the hospital's newborn mortality rate showed a sudden increase. Perfectly healthy babies had died without apparent cause. Medical examiners were called in to study the phenomenon. They reviewed each case trying to find some clue. Tests were conducted, procedures reviewed and then reviewed again. There was nothing to explain the mysterious rise in infant deaths.

Then one day, one of the examiners made an offhand observation about the nursery personnel: "You seem to be short-handed on the third shift," he said.

The hospital administrator explained that an elderly woman, a nurse's aide, had retired and not been replaced. "Mother Dora was something of a fixture around here," the executive explained. "She loved babies and took care of them as if they were her own. No baby cried for long without being picked up and cuddled and sung to when Dora was on duty."

"And now?" asked the examiner.

"Well, the babies probably aren't held as much. Could it be . . . ?"

The next day a notice went up on the nursery bulletin board: **Beginning today, all babies are to be held a minimum of ten minutes each hour.**

And the problem went away.[12]

While this seems to be an isolated case, surprisingly, its findings have been seen all around the world. Can science prove to us that babies can sense love? Well, science has shown that babies can sense a lack of love. A baby who is unwanted by its mother will not feed well when given either breast or bottle milk by the mother. Yet, if the baby is given to a nurse who loves, cuddles, and holds the baby close, we notice the baby feeds well. Babies, therefore, do feel a deficit of love at a very early age, and if a baby can sense that lack of love, how much more so does an older child?

> *If a baby can sense a lack of love, how much more so does an older child sense that lack of love?*

Children are quick to perceive when love is insufficient and react with such behaviors as insecurity, resentment, jealousy, and even hatred. Children dislike being told they are bad and have no worth. Some children have been told so often they are useless that they try to live up to their reputation. Someone has well said, "Faults are always thick where love is thin."[13]

> *When we truly love a child, and when he knows this, serious discipline problems are much less likely to arise.*

Here is the point: Children need to be loved. This is the first paintbrush of three we use to paint our masterpiece. We have seen that God as a parent loves His children. God has put love into the heart of every parent as well. Why has He set this example and made these provisions in parents? Because children need to be loved. They need to be caressed; they need to be comforted. Even the newborn baby is clearly comforted by being held in his mother's arms and experiencing the tender care that is normally afforded him. When we truly love a child, and when he knows this, serious discipline problems are much less likely to arise. We work so hard at "parenting" our older children that we sometimes forget to love and enjoy them as we should.

How to Express Love to Your Child

Gary Chapman has written a wonderful book entitled *The Five Love Languages*.[15] In this book he categorizes love into five basic areas: physical touch, words of affirmation, quality time, acts of service, and giving of gifts. The book is primarily written to help men and women discover the primary love language in their spouse. However, this technique may also help you in expressing love to your children.

The principle is that all human beings have a particular love language. If you want to show love to a person, you must find out which love language it is for them. You cannot depend on *your* feelings, only *their* feelings. Just because you feel more accepted when people spend quality time with you, this may not be what your husband likes. He may value time by himself. His love language may be, and probably is, words of affirmation. You may be going out of your way to spend time with him, to make him feel loved, when what he really wants is for you to affirm him. See the importance.

Now it is difficult to determine exactly to which type your child responds best. Therefore, Gary Chapman says to "Pour them all on." I agree with this. In fact, in questioning others about their love language, I have discovered something very important. Most people's love language in the adult years is determined by what they did not receive as a child. For instance, a child who does not receive much physical touch usually grows up wanting to be touched. A child whose father never spent much time with him greatly values a person who spends time with him later in life. Let's take a minute and look at these five areas in dealing with your child.

• Physical Touch

We have already said how important it is that your child receive touch. This is initially the best way to communicate love to your baby. Don't stop. Keep it going. I love to see a teenage son and his father hug. Your growing child may go through stages where he pushes you away. Don't take that as a rejection. He may just be trying to hide this action from his peers. Most children, deep down, still want it to continue. Always make it available.

Children need and desire this physical touch. My grandson, Jack, will walk over to me and with one motion throw his arms straight into the air and says in sweet tender tones, "Hold chew!" I will gladly respond by picking him up and holding him close to my heart. In my opinion, there's nothing better.

If you find your child loving to wrestle and climb all over you, chances are that his love language is touch. Be sensitive to that and respond appropriately.

A very close doctor friend of mine could have certainly been categorized as an unlovable person. He was crass, overbearing, and rude. He had the capability of making everyone under his authority fear him. He could make his nurses cry with a single comment. One of my nurses brought to my attention a justification for this doctor's behavior. She was having dinner with him when the doctor made the comment, "I never can remember my mother ever hugging me." This nurse of mine just sat there and cried.

• Words of Affirmation

Make it a habit to tell your children every day that you love them. I remember my son and I used to play a little game. I would go to him and say, "Son, you know what I haven't done this morning?"

Make it a habit to tell your children every day that you love them.

"What, Dad?" "I haven't told you that I love you." A little bit later he would say to me, "Dad, do you know what I haven't done since noon today?" "What?" "I haven't told you that I love you." It was great. Sometimes we would race to see which one could express his love first.

Tell your child you love him. How else is a child to know of his parent's love unless you tell him?

A father brought his teenage son to my office because of severe discipline problems. In the discussion I asked the father, "When have you told your seventeen-year-old son that you love him?" He said, "I never have." Fewer discipline problems occur when the child knows his parents love him and make him feel special.

There are other ways you may affirm your child—and you should use those. But most of all, tell him every day, "I love you."

• Time

We will devote many pages to quality time in the chapters to come. There is a horribly inaccurate saying that is going around: "It is not the quantity of time that is important, it is the quality of time." This simply is wrong. Children can quickly sense when you have scheduled time. It doesn't matter what you do with them, just be there. Chances are when they grow up, they will not remember where you went or what you did with them. They will remember how much time you gave them. Quantity supersedes quality. Don't let anyone tell you otherwise. Patrick Morley has well said, "Availability is more important than structure. It is not the mistakes we make with them that devastate their lives; it is the neglect."[16]

• Acts of Service

There will be some children who will be sensitive to your acts of service. They will see your cooking, cleaning, and caring for them as a signal that you love them. I will warn you, most children take this for granted. You can occasionally remind them that you care for their needs because you love them. My granddaughter, Mary Grace, loves to perform acts of service toward her little brother. She will take him his bottle, bring his blanket to him, or correct him verbally when he gets out of line. Much of this is her attempt to imitate Mommy, but it is also a demonstration of love through acts of service toward her brother in a manner that she feels from her Mommy. Children whose primary love language is acts of service will respond gratefully.

• Giving of Gifts

With children, you have to be very careful with this one. Everyone loves to receive gifts. That does not make this a primary love language. Don't ever get the idea that money can buy love. They are completely unrelated. "Money will buy a fine dog, but only love will make him wag his tail."[17] Money can never replace a parent's love and accessibility. Children need guidance and understanding, not just a house key and a car key.

It is my opinion that giving gifts should mainly be reserved for special days such as Christmas, birthdays, and other related holidays. On these days honor them with gifts. Make a huge deal out of birthdays. This is one of the best days to communicate love to your child. Now this does not mean you shouldn't give your child a "happy" every once in a while. However, your child will soon realize that it does not mean that he will walk out with a gift every time he walks into the store.

By limiting gifts to special days, you are sending a message to your child that love cannot be bought. You see, you will have to use one of the other methods to communicate your love for all of the other days of the year. This way the child learns that he has the capability to love others even with a bankrupt piggy bank. Children between four and five years of age are very open and sensitive to the teachings of parents. These teaching concepts often become permanent at these ages.

Love Languages with Multiple Siblings

I have seen time and time again children grow up in the same family under the same conditions when one child feels loved and the other does not. Why is this? Oftentimes the parents have loved in one or two of the five areas and have avoided the others. It just so happens that one child's primary love language was met by the parents, but the other child's love language was avoided. When they are children, pour all five on thick.

Playing Favorites

Of course, you should never have a favorite child. Oftentimes the middle child will struggle with a feeling of lesser value than the older and younger sibling. This is usually caused because the oldest child is recognized for being the first to do everything. The youngest child is often treated more like a grandchild. Consequently, the middle child does not receive much attention. If this is your scenario, be sensitive to it. Make special opportunities just for the middle child that will give him a moment under the spotlight.

How should you respond when your child asks which child you love best?

When the small daughter of the distinguished sculptress Sally Farnham was once asked which child was her mother's favorite, the little girl promptly replied, "She loves Jimmy best because he's the oldest, and she loves Johnny best because he's the youngest, and she loves me best because I'm the only girl."[18]

I believe this is sort of the way God does it. He loves us all best. He loves us all equally and individually. This is what we should model before our children.

Fathers and mothers should try to have "Date Nights" individually with each child. This helps to teach your children they are special and that you have reserved time specifically for them. This is a great way to show them the attention they need.

Mom and Dad's Love

We have already talked about the importance of a mother's love in the family, and the effects of a father's love in the home, but what about their love for one another? Does that produce anything of importance for children? You can bet the farm it does!

A strong marriage between a husband and a wife is vital to a child's understanding of God's design for the family. I was so blessed to be raised in a family where divorce was never a possibility. I have never in my life heard the word "divorce" even threatened in the relationship between my mom and dad. This provides great security in the home.

This world is rough. There are very few places of refuge and shelter. The home should be a sanctuary and haven for peace. Unfortunately, this is lacking in so many homes—but it doesn't have to be in yours.

Parade before your children a float of unconditional and sacrificial love for your spouse.

Fathers, make your home peaceful. The best way to do that is to love your wife. It has been said that the best way to compliment your wife is frequently.[19] Parade before your children a float of unconditional and sacrificial love for your spouse. Be so, so careful what you let your child see. Try your best to remove arguments and division between you and your mate from the eyes and ears of your children. This is one of the most important things you can do to establish your home: Love your spouse.

Eve asked Adam one day, "Adam, do you love me?" Adam responded, "Who else?"[20]

We need more children to grow up to say, "My daddy had eyes only for my mom"; "I know that my daddy loves my mom"; "The concept of my parents' getting a divorce has never entered my mind"; "My home is secure." Parents, what your children will ultimately say lies in your hands today.

Can You Love Your Child Too Much?

The answer in a nutshell: YES!! I often have mothers who come into the office and express that the only form of discipline needed in their home is love. One mother's note read,

> My fifteen-month-old daughter will, at times, "slap" me when I'm holding her and something she doesn't like happens (as I tell her "No" or I don't pay enough attention to her, or tell her it's time for bed). Also, she bangs her head on the floor during tantrums. I need ideas on non-corporal discipline measures.

Her last sentence tied my hands. Her child needs more than love.

There will be a more in-depth section on this during the chapters on disciplining, but this would certainly be a case where too much love prevents a parent from disciplining properly.

I have had other mothers who have an unhealthy love for their child. One mother was so concerned that her child would get sick that she would give him an aspirin every day. This is very destructive to a child's stomach. I repeatedly told her not to do this, but she felt that her child needed it. It was not long until I was treating the child for severe stomach ulcers.

A parent's love for his child also can cause a pediatrician to go insane. I'm referring to middle-of-the-night phone calls. I realize that there are emergencies that need my attention at all hours. I am happy to respond to such incidents. But when I graduated from medical school I had no idea that a mother's love blinds her common sense. One of my favorite recollections, even though I was not pleased at the time, occurred at about 1:00 a.m. The phone rang and the voice on the phone was a young mother. She said, "Dr. Slonecker, my baby just cut his first tooth. When do I brush it?" Remember, this was at 1:00 a.m. If I had been more alert I would have sarcastically told her, knowing that the Farmer's Market was the only store open all night back then, that she had to have a special medicated toothpaste and it had to be done within the next forty-five minutes. However, I was not that coherent, nor brilliant, coming out of a sound sleep. There have been other phone calls to rattle my patience. I have been awakened several times at 3:00 a.m. to hear on the other end of the line a mother's voice asking, "What time does the office open?"

Getting back to our topic: Can you love your child too much? Absolutely. You can love him too much to discipline him properly. You can love him to an unhealthy point. You may also love him to the point where it blocks your common sense. There is one other area where too much love is harmful. You can spoil your child with love. When a child learns that love will prevent his mom and dad from acting against what he does, then the child takes advantage of it. Children can get away with murder in their home. They get everything they want. It has been well said, "Spoiled kids soon become little stinkers."[21]

Love In Action

One mother who had children who were remarkable examples of early piety was asked the secret of her success. She answered,

While my children were infants on my lap, as I washed them, I raised my heart to God, that he would wash them in that blood which cleanseth from all sin; as I clothed them in the morning, I asked my Heavenly Father to clothe them with the robe of Christ's righteousness; as I provided them food, I prayed that God would feed their souls with the bread of heaven, and give them to drink of the water of life. When I have prepared them for the house of God, I have pleaded that their bodies might be fit temples for the Holy Ghost to dwell in. When they left me for the week-day school, I followed their infant footsteps with a prayer, that their path through life might be like that of the just, which shineth more and more unto the perfect day. And as I committed them to the rest of the night, the silent breathing of my soul has been, that their Heavenly Father would take them to his embrace, and fold them in his paternal arms.[22]

Praying for your children is one of the best ways to show that you love them. This woman's love for her children oozed from her heart to the heart of God. She wanted the best for her children because she loved them. She knew that the best was not to be found in earthly pleasures, but in heavenly treasures. She sought God to make them the persons that He wanted them to be.

As we have mentioned before, love is not the only brush used in the masterpiece, although it is a crucial one. It is one of the big three. You see, love will drive parents to take action to train their child. Without love, many of the other responsibilities of rearing fall by the wayside. I want to close this chapter with a poem entitled "I Loved You Enough," written by an unknown author. It encapsulates this idea of the foundational nature of love that other parenting techniques can be built upon.

Someday when my children are old enough to understand the logic that motivates a parent, I will tell them: I loved you enough to ask where you were going, with whom, and what time you

would be home. I loved you enough to insist that you save your money and buy a bike for yourself even though we could afford to buy one for you. I loved you enough to be silent and let you discover that your new best friend was a creep. I loved you enough to make you take a Milky Way back to the drugstore (with a bite out of it) and tell the clerk, "I stole this yesterday and want to pay for it." I loved you enough to stand over you for two hours while you cleaned your room, a job that would have taken me fifteen minutes. I loved you enough to let you see anger, disappointment and tears in my eyes. Children must learn that their parents aren't perfect. I loved you enough to let you assume the responsibility for your actions even when the penalties were so harsh they almost broke my heart. But most of all, I loved you enough to say NO when I knew you would hate me for it. Those were the most difficult battles of all. I'm glad I won them, because in the end, you won something too.[23]

This kind of love NEVER fails!

Chapter 4

"Who's the Boss?"

Remember at the close of Chapter Two, I mentioned a canal that had three guiding lights for the captains. If those captains would visually position their vessels so as to make those three lights one, they could be assured of safe passage through the canal. We have discussed one of those beacons of light in parenting. It is love. The second of those three lights is authority. It is our second paintbrush used to paint our masterpiece.

There are two rails for any train track. They always run side by side. Where there is one, you will always find the other. If one turns right, the other turns right at the same point. If the land takes

> *If at any point along the track one rail is missing, disaster results.*

one to a higher plain, the other is sure to be there right by its side. If the valleys bring that track to lower depths, you can be sure both rails will head down. If at any point along the track one rail is missing, disaster results. This is the special relationship that love and authority have with each other. If you have love and no authority, or if you have authority without love, your train is sure to wreck. It takes both, all the time, in every situation.

This chapter is intended to help you understand some general principles regarding authority. Again, in this chapter we are trying to establish the ideal. This is what to shoot for. Many of the practical techniques for reestablishing authority in a rebellious household will be in the following chapters. Nevertheless, it is very important to understand the ideal. This helps you shoot for excellence—something we should do in all things. I have divided this material into six sections: the **Product** of no authority, the **Purpose** of proper authority, the **Pressures** against all authority, the **Participants** in parental authority, the **Pollution** of improper authority, and the **Potential** of regaining authority.

The Product of No Authority: When Authority Is Missing

I received a phone call one evening from a frantic mother who needed help. She told me that her son had a high fever. When I asked what the child's temperature was, she replied that her child would not let her take his temperature. I immediately thought perhaps her son was the fullback for the Tennessee Titans, but when I asked her the age of her son, she said, "Two weeks of age." If this mother does not have enough authority over her two-week-old baby to take his temperature, what will she be dealing with when her child enters the teen-age years?

Another mother called the office to schedule an appointment for her sick child. We told her that it would be fine to bring the child in right away. She replied, "I have to wait until after it quits raining." We curiously asked, "Why?" She responded, "The child is afraid of the windshield wipers." Doesn't that make you want to ask the question, "Just who is in authority?"

Again, Dr. Donald Grey Barnhouse, one of my favorite illustrators, has another enlightening story.

> *In a large hotel, I heard a mother ask her five-year-old child if she might leave the table in order to go and see someone across the room. She explained that she would be back in a moment. The child answered with a blatant, "No." The mother asked pleadingly two or three times more, and the child said, "No, if you go, I'll not eat my meal at all today." The mother sat there helpless; by her own lack of discipline she had created a monster who now ruled her.[1]*

Are you beginning to see the importance of authority? Without it, managing your children will be chaotic. Without authority, you will become frustrated, confused, and angry. It will seem as though everything you try will fail. When you are given authority of any kind at any age, it must be guarded carefully because if you lose it, it will be very hard to ever get back.

Tom said to his mother, "Mom, I don't want to go to school today." His mom asked, "Why not?" Tom explained, "Because the kids laugh and make fun of me." "But Tom," exclaimed his mom, "you have to go. You're the principal."

Authority is something given to you by God when you become a parent. But it can be lost, and when it is, it makes parenting very difficult. In fact, it can be impossible.

As I entered the treatment room, I asked the child to climb up on the table. To my surprise, this four-year-old cursed me out. He went on and on and on—words that made an old sailor look like a saint. Now remember, he was only four years old. I looked at his mother, who was now rather embarrassed, and asked her what she was going to do. She said, "We'll have to take care of that when we get home." This incorrigible child then turned on his mother and let out a string of words that would make the devil himself blush. I told the mother, "I wouldn't wait till I got home," and then I walked out of the treatment room to give her the opportunity to rectify the situation.

This experience did not altogether surprise me. I knew this family well and understood what was going on. The husband was never home, and oftentimes neither was the mom. The children fended for themselves. They had a live-in nanny who cared for the children on a day-to-day basis. The children had absolutely no authority in their lives. And by the way, where does a four-year-old get his vocabulary? Mainly from his parents. To this day, this mother still has no control over her children. I am fearful of what these children will become, perhaps, like many other children today: criminals with absolutely no respect for authority.

The Purpose of Proper Authority: When Authority Is Mastered

I trust these stories give you a glimpse of what you don't want to have in parenting. But what do you want? Most of us would say that we would like to have a child who is obedient. You see, if you have an obedient child, then you can teach your child your principles and expect him to follow. What is the key to obedience? It is simple—AUTHORITY!

> *What is the key to obedience? It is simple—Authority!*

God has put authority over us in many areas of our life. Government, for instance, is an institution established by God for us and in authority over us. The Bible says in Romans 13:1, "Let every soul be subject to the governing authorities. For there is no authority except from God, and the authorities that exist are appointed by God." God appoints authority. He has appointed parents to have authority over their children.

> *Children, obey your parents in the Lord, for this is right. "Honor your father and mother," which is the first commandment with promise: "that it may be well with you and you may live long on the earth."*
>
> *Ephesians 6:1-3*

Other than God himself, the only other authority given in the Ten Commandments is parental. But why? Why is parental authority so very, very important? Well, authority teaches obedience. A person learns obedience when he is a child. He learns to obey from his parents first. God is an authority, as well. He is the ultimate authority. He desires obedience from His children, too. Therefore, **(now here is the key)** the message a child learns about authority when he is young will have a dramatic effect upon his understanding of God's authority later on in life. If a child learns the importance of being obedient to his parents, a child will have an easier time respecting God as an authority and being obedient to His commands. If a child learns that disobedience carries penalties as a child, that child will also know that disobeying God carries with it penalties as well. This principle is called building the fear of the Lord in your child.

The message the child learns about authority when he is young will have a dramatic effect upon his understanding of God's authority later on in life.

Psalm 111:10 says, "The fear of the LORD is the beginning of wisdom; a good understanding have all those who do His commandments." This fear is an awesome, reverent respect for God's authority. When is it built? It is fashioned within the relationship of a parent and a child over the understanding of authority. If you desire your child to be wise, teach him to obey authority. The beginning of wisdom is fear of the Lord.

Now we have the answer—the purpose of proper authority is to put the fear of the Lord in our children. But what is proper authority? I believe that it is wrapped up in the commandment, "Honor your father and your mother." This is the only commandment in Scripture directly given to children. "Children, obey your parents." It cannot be any clearer, but oftentimes we need an example. How about Jesus?

Was Jesus a child who obeyed His parents? Yes. In Luke 2:51 the Bible says, "Then He [Jesus] went down with them [Mary and Joseph] and came to Nazareth, and was subject to them." Jesus was subject to His parents. Another way of saying this is, Jesus was obedient to His parents. In fact, many translations use the word *obedient*.

Interestingly enough, this verse comes right after Jesus was found at twelve years of age teaching in the synagogue. Being twelve carried special significance in the Jewish culture. It meant that Jesus had entered manhood. If at any time it was appropriate to cut the apron strings, it would be then. Yet Jesus continued to obey His parents. He was subject to them even after His manhood had arrived. The way this is written in the Greek denotes habitual continuous obedience. They were His parents and He would honor them all the days of His life.

Now this brings up an interesting point. Your authority as a parent over your child never ends. While your responsibility decreases as the years pass, your authority does not. While their independence expands, your authority still remains. Don't get the idea that your authority shrinks as they grow into adulthood. They should still honor you and value you. Being a parent is a responsibility given to you by God as a lifetime position. Children may be smarter than you. They may achieve greater positions in life, but you are still their parents. Don't let them tell you they know more, or consequently you will cease to have authority over them. Christ was one Child who knew more than His parents, yet He obeyed them.[2]

> *The litmus test of authority is obedience.*

The litmus test of authority is obedience. Does your child obey you? If so, then he respects you as an authority. If not, then you need to establish who the authority is. Someone has well said, "The time to teach obedience to authority is in the playpen instead of the state pen."[3]

If you tell your child to do something, authority makes sure that it is done. He may not like it, but authority is not negotiable.

Do you have it? The purpose of proper authority is to teach obedience. This obedience is initially given to the parents, but later it is transferred to God. This is placing the fear of the Lord in your child, which is the beginning of all wisdom.

The Pressures Against All Authority: When Authority Is Movable

A twelve-year-old child told his mother, "My job is to get away with as much as I can, and your job is to stop me." Just as though it seems rules were made to be broken, authority was made to be tested. The question is not what do you do **if** authority is challenged, but **when** it is challenged.

In this day and age, you can bank on it: Your authority will be tested by your child. If your authority is movable, you will fail as a parent. If your child knows that his charm, cunning, and craftiness can impel you to change your mind, he will use it every time. Your authority must be immovable and unchangeable.

Parents have a tougher task these days. Dr. James Dobson said in his newsletter, "In previous centuries teens were capable of resisting authority—but the culture didn't bait them to do it."[4] In the sixties we had rebels with a cause. In the nineties we have rebels without a cause. They are rebelling and they don't even know why. One teenager who was buying some shoes asked the salesman, "If my parents like these shoes, may I bring them back?"[5] Rebels without a cause: They have MTV as their parents and their punishment is governed by the liberal judicial system that protects the criminal more than the victim.

In the sixties we had rebels with a cause. In the nineties we have rebels without a cause.

I relate all of that to say this: Children today need godly authority in their lives. You, as their parents, have been given this task. Now you know why one parent said, "The accent may be on youth, but the stress is still on the parents."[6] God has given you the position of authority. Maintain this authority with inflexible barriers to rebellion. Be like the mother in the following story.

> In a hotel, I watched a mother tell her child to come inside. The child, about two or three years old, rebelled with no uncertain terms and gestures. The mother said nothing and started toward the stairs. The child came inside and stamped her feet. The mother continued on upstairs and out of sight. The crying child went to the foot of the stairs, and started slowly up, stopping occasionally to stamp and cry louder. The mother was nowhere to be seen. I followed the child; eventually she reached the top of the stairs, turned down the hall and entered the room.[7]

Strong, immovable, untestable authority will solve your potential rebellions. As Barney Fife used to say, "It nips it in the bud."

The Participants in Parental Authority: When Authority Is Multiplied

> When my child is with his grandparents, they change the rules, and don't do what they say they are going to do. They are not firm and even provoke him with obnoxious teasing!!!
> —Mother of a six-year-old

> He would rather stay at grandmother's. Sometimes, because she'll hold him all the time, and won't spank when needed. She doesn't believe much in spanking, but lets him hit her. We do NOT allow that.
> —Mother of six-month-old and a two-and-a-half-year-old

Bob Orben jokes about the chain of authority within the family. He says, "Have you noticed that when children misbehave, they always seem to go through the family legal system—Mom is the prosecutor, Dad the judge, and Grandmother the Court of Last Appeals."[8]

As a parent, one of your responsibilities is to share authority over your child with other individuals. These figures are represented in baby-sitters, school teachers, day care workers, and the church nursery personnel. However, in some families, this balance of authority is most difficult in dealing with grandparents.

The doorbell rang. Jimmy went to answer it. "Mom! There's a man at the door collecting for the old folks' home. Shall I give him Grandma?"

Let's take a minute and examine the role and responsibility of a grandparent. The parent carries the ultimate responsibility for the child's behavior. Therefore, the parents' style and standards should be reinforced by the grandparents.

Grandmoms and Granddads, your role is to support your children in their unique manner of parenting. Now I know this is difficult. Your style of parenting probably raised perfectly well-behaved and successful children. You think your grown children are parenting all wrong. It is very frustrating, but still, your children will have to answer for their own actions. I'll say it again: Your role as a grandparent is to support your children.

Parents, make sure that you give the grandparents the authority to back up your discipline techniques. If you use painful punishment when authority is tested, make sure the grandparents have the permission to do the same. Usually, discipline from grandparents should be held to a minimum. The child will not normally test the authority of the grandparents as often as that of the parents, but sooner or later, it will be tested. Make sure they have the authority from you to exercise proper discipline.

Grandparents have a unique role with their grandchildren. Many of them like to spoil their grandchildren. Grandparents want them to have everything. Spoiling your grandchild is acceptable to a point. You will not only be able to spoil him with gifts and rewards, but you can spoil him with time. You may give your grandchild your undivided attention—something that parents cannot usually do. Children love this. Grandparents can take them places and give them special opportunities that parents simply do not have time for nor have the extra income to provide.

Parents, you make the rules, not the grandparents. Nevertheless, if you are a wise parent you will listen to the wisdom of your parents.

They have been there. They know what works and what does not. Respect their opinions. Continue to honor them. Give them full authority to discipline your children. Ask graciously for them to uphold your standards and to aid in training your children.

Grandparents are vital assets for a child. The following appeared in *Family Circle* and was written by Mrs. Jonas E. Salk:

> *Older people's participation in our lives gives our children a sense of continuity—a sense of generations, of the flow and ebb of life. This perspective is one that children absorb: A realization that age means experience, that age need not be feared; a dim recognition that parents, too, were once children. Today we have suburban developments where children of young families are growing up without seeing old people as part of their day-to-day living. It seems to me that children need the natural balance of both young and old—and contact with their grandparents helps to provide this.*[9]

A Word of Advice Concerning Other Authorities

From time to time you will find the need to leave your child with other adults for supervision. Here is the rule of thumb to follow if it is possible. Don't leave your child with anyone whom you cannot trust enough to discipline your child properly, and certainly don't leave him with someone who doesn't care enough to discipline him at all. When you leave your child with someone you trust, give that person the full authority to discipline. In some special cases, when trust is rock solid, you may give the freedom to that person to exercise painful punishment. Before doing this, make sure you know this person very well. Give him as much authority as he deserves.

Don't leave your child with anyone whom you cannot trust enough to discipline your child properly, and certainly don't leave him with someone who doesn't care enough to discipline him at all.

After you have given him this authority, stand behind his actions. Don't undermine his authority by taking up for the child. For instance, your child may get in trouble at school. Don't get angry at the school system. The understanding with my children was that if they got in trouble at school, they were going to get in more trouble at home. My wife and I supported the school officials in whose care we had placed them. They knew that they were to obey them as if they were their parents.

Your child will potentially try to falsify the truth; that is, he will lie concerning what really happened. One child came home from his first day of school with a note from his teacher pinned to his clothes. It read, "If you promise not to believe everything your child says happens at school, I'll promise not to believe everything he says happens at home."

Whether they are baby-sitters, school teachers, nursery workers, or relatives, give them as much authority over your child as they deserve. Then stand behind them when they are forced to discipline your child. They are providing a valuable service for you. They need your support.

The Pollution of Improper Authority: When Authority Is Misused

Remember we said that if authority is to be in its proper position, it must be balanced with love. A whole category of unsuccessful parents have taken authority to the extreme and sacrificed love as a result. "Authority is like a bank account. The more you draw on it, the less you have."[10] Authority is something given to you just because you are a parent. Respecting that authority is something earned by your daily interaction with your child. If it is misused, respect for you and your authority will decline. Rebellion will begin in your child. Unfortunately, that rebellion will continue in his life against every authority that he encounters.

• Authority is Persuasive

Respect for authority means influence. Your children are watching your actions and emulating them. The following is a true account that unfolded in a steel mill in Gary, Indiana.

This man was a reckless fellow and a gambler. One day as molten iron was being poured from a furnace, he gathered a group of men and bet each one of them five dollars that he could take his naked finger and whip it rapidly through the inch-thick stream of fiery iron. They all covered his bet. He stooped to the floor, took up a handful of the powdery dust all around the furnace and used it to dry all the body oil from his finger. Coating his finger with this hot, dry dust, he thrust it at the liquid iron and caused the sparks to fly in many directions. Another workman watched the incident, went down to another place in the mill where a similar stream of iron was flowing and bet a group of men that he could whip his finger through the molten metal. They, likewise, covered his bet, and he whipped his finger through the stream of metal. But he did not know the secret of wiping the body oil from the finger with the parched dust. They took him to the first-aid station where a surgeon removed his entire finger.[11]

Before you act, think who is watching. You have knowledge that your children do not have. You have experience that they do not have. Don't use your position of knowledge in a way that will bring harm to your children. Your actions will chart the direction that they will travel.

• **Authority is Prideful**

We all want perfect children. The reality is, your children will have times of disobedience and rebellion. That is only natural. We are all born sinners, even children. Now, authority often carries with it a reputation. Parents like to compare themselves to others. The danger comes when parents are in public with their children. Parents want to impress others with their children's remarkable obedience. Oftentimes the parents unjustly punish the children for something that they are incapable of understanding.

For instance, a two-year-old

The parents need to consider what is going on in the child's mind before they consider their own reputation or what others will think.

should not be taken to a two-hour meeting where he is forced to sit in a seat and not move. This demand is too difficult to accomplish. Yet so many parents try this. Then, when their child cries or misbehaves, he gets a pop on the leg. Oftentimes the parents are looking over their shoulders to see who saw this. The parents need to consider what is going on in the child's mind before they consider their own reputation or what others will think. Be wise up front and don't put your child in situations where expectations supersede his ability. Furthermore, when these situations do arise, lay aside your parental pride and do what is best for the child.

• **Authority is Powerful**

Herod was a powerful man with a great deal of authority. It was said that when he ordered the slaying of the infants of Bethlehem, his own son was not excluded from the list. When Augustus Caesar heard of this action in Rome, he said, "It was better to be Herod's pig than his son."[12] For you see, Jews were not allowed to eat the flesh of pigs; therefore, the pigs could die a natural death.

> *When authority is thought of as power, it is most often abused.*

When authority is thought of as power, it is most often abused. Many parents try to instill obedience into their children by domination—authority is thick and love is thin.

One patient of mine was scared to death of his parents. At first, I considered physical abuse, but knowing the parents so well, I ruled that out, and did so correctly. It was a classic case of too much authority in the home. When a child comes into a doctor's office for a physical, you expect him to cry. He is cold, naked, with strangers, and usually being stuck with things that hurt. The father of this child refused to let his son cry. I typically enjoy grabbing a hug from a child before he leaves. This child would first look at his father to make sure it was okay. He was a little boy with a crushed spirit. The mother's number one complaint: "I can't stand for him to whine." She would use harsh measures to get this natural characteristic that appears in all children out of her son.

I spoke at length with his parents about their abuse of authority. I felt that there was still a chance to renew this child's spirit. Through encouragement and an abundance of love, he could be restored. Otherwise, I felt he was being set up for an upscale rebellion.

His parents were wonderful people. They wanted what was best for him. In fact, they were aiming for the perfect child. Unfortunately, they were using the powerful force found in authority to accomplish this. It will not work. It takes love and authority in proper balance. I am happy to say that the parents responded with love and affection. I have seen remarkable improvement!

The Potential of Regaining Authority: When Authority Is Manufactured

If you feel as though you have lost your authority with your child, there is hope. It can be regained, but it takes a lot of work. Most of these techniques have been reserved for the chapters ahead, but I want to give you an encouraging example before we close this chapter.

As I entered the treatment room, I found a four-year-old little boy and his frustrated mother. The disturbed, weakened mother looked helplessly at me and exclaimed, "I can't control him one bit. He throws these temper tantrums all of the time and there is nothing I can do to get him to quit." I responded, "Nothing!" And she replied, "Absolutely nothing!!" I told her that it sounded to me as if her son was in the driver's seat and that she was in the back seat. She agreed and responded, "That is exactly what it looks like. But can you help me?"

The problem was, she must regain the authority. But how? I explained to her, "The next time that he has a temper tantrum at home, get up and go to the next room. He will get up and follow you and have another tantrum in that room. Get up and go to the third room. Your son will follow, where he will repeat the process. You have given him three opportunities to get over his anger without your interfering. However, should the child come into the third room and have another tantrum, then I, as a parent, would give him something to have a temper tantrum about. The time would have come to administer some painful love licks on his backside."

When I said this, the boy was still in the room. He perked up and listened intently. He knew exactly what he had been doing, and he didn't like the doctor's suggestion.

A few days later, the mother called to thank me for my advice. She said that it had worked very well, and she had started the move from the back seat to the front seat.

There you have it. Don't lose hope. I realize this chapter painted the ideal. I hope it is not too late with your child to go for the best. Pursue excellence in parenting. More practical suggestions for regaining authority will be in the pages to come. Stay tuned. What we need to grasp firmly, for now, is that authority is just one of three of the paintbrushes used to paint your masterpiece.

Chapter 5

Can Your Kids Trust You?

The righteous man walks in his integrity; his children are blessed after him.

PROVERBS 20:7

As we have seen so far, three ingredients are needed in balanced amounts in the recipe for successful parenting. The first is LOVE. We looked at the importance of developing an unconditional love for your child that will never fail. The second ingredient is AUTHORITY. We discussed the child's need for a firm authority that enforces boundaries and maintains the standards. Now we have reached the third component—TRUST. Of the three, this is often the most neglected. It is

> *Trust is the missing link in the chain of parenting.*

the missing link in the chain of parenting. This is our third paintbrush used to paint our masterpiece: the brush that is the most expensive because of its ability to create details. It is also costly because if ever lost or destroyed, it is the most difficult to replace.

Trust is, perhaps, the most difficult to achieve. You see, love most of the time comes naturally. All you must do is nurture it. Authority is a position. All that you have to do is maintain the respect. But trust—this is something altogether different. Trust has to be earned. Plus, if it is ever lost, it takes a great deal of time and effort to restore it. It is never an easy fix.

The supreme paradox of childhood is that children desire to be led by their parents but insist that they earn the right to lead them. This chapter is devoted to help you in your endeavors to earn that right. We will first try to gain a better understanding of the importance of trust between a parent and a child. Then we will look at some trust-busters and some trust-builders.

What is Trust?

My younger son, Chris, had an experience that defines trust. I want him to tell it to you in his own words.

Not too long ago, I had the distinct privilege, reserved mainly for youth ministers, of co-leading a college ski trip to Colorado. What a sacrifice—I know. Now I had never been skiing before and was really looking forward to it. Little did I know what awaited me.

It would be safe to say that I am not a Type A personality; just ask anyone who knows me. My adrenal glands are rather tame. They do not have fits of massive adrenaline release that require me to jump out of an airplane four thousand feet above the ground, leap off a cliff with a springy cord attached to my ankle, or glide through the Grand Canyon on a kite one thousand feet above the ground. I like life; I enjoy living. I have no plans to get that close to death, especially on purpose. That doesn't excite me. I am just not put together like that.

But here I was, my debut on the slopes. I should have known that this was not for me when I put my skis on for the first time. I stood up in the parking lot and fell over. For the next ten minutes I desperately tried to get my feet into a position that was under me and parallel again so that I could resume my vertical stance. Then my wife led me to this massively steep and intimidating slope. To me it looked more like a cliff. We punched our tickets and boarded the lift to take us up to the top of the course, humiliatingly and improperly called the "Bunny Slope."

Skiing was not as hard as I thought; it was much harder. It took me hours to get down the slopes. As I would work my way back and forth across the mountain, I would see the same people who had been down three times since I started, and they had gotten lunch in between. To me, falling was enjoyable. I was never going fast enough to get hurt, and at least when I was on the ground my muscles could relax from the tension. I was a basket of nerves.

Through the week, I somewhat improved; at least that is what people were telling me. I progressed from the bunny slope, to the green slopes, and had even attempted some blues. Now I can assure you, the speed police would have never warned me on any of these. I looked more like I was strolling through the park, rather than downhill skiing. I never got over being petrified. I just knew that at any moment my skis would get perfectly parallel on a turn and I would freeze. I saw myself time and time again flying down the mountain to my death. Hence, I was overly cautious.

Then to my amazement, I saw the most incredible thing. I was having one of my communions with the snow (I had fallen down again) when I heard a man's voice. He was yelling, "Right!" then "Left!" then "Right!" again. I turned around and saw a skier with a bright orange vest on (the vest was to indicate that he was blind). Behind him was the voice that I had heard calling in the air. He was the blind man's guide. They both came whizzing by me as they sped down the mountain. The blind man seemed to be as calm and at peace as I would be walking in the park. I just sat there in amazement.

This gave me great confidence. I thought if this blind man can do it, so can I. I spent a few minutes and tried to psych myself up. I jumped to my feet (well not really, it was more like I stumbled to my feet) and prepared to take control of this mountain. I started off really well, saying to myself, "Right, Left, Right." I began to pick up speed. Faster and faster I traveled. Then it happened: My right ski hit a patch of ice, and my face slammed into the snow. Thank the good Lord, snow is soft.

When I reached the bottom, I began to reflect upon the blind skier that I had witnessed. Here was a man who had put total trust in the guide behind him. To him, that trust meant the difference between enjoyment and disaster. He had trusted the guide with his life. Wow, what a picture of trust.

Trust is not just agreeing with someone about what you think will work. It is not a decision that both of you come to the same conclusion about. It is releasing your control and letting him make the decision for you. It is a total reliance upon another.

Why Is Trust So Important?

Trust is going to help you as a parent master two domains with your child. First, if your child trusts you, he is more likely to obey you.

Second, if trust is developed, his confidence in you as his leader will blossom.

• **Trust enhances obedience.**

In How Life Imitates the World Series, *Thomas Boswell tells a story about Earl Weaver, former manager of the Baltimore Orioles. Sports fans will enjoy how he handled star Reggie Jackson.*

Weaver had a rule that no one could steal a base unless given the steal sign. This upset Jackson because he felt he knew the pitchers and catchers well enough to judge who he could and could not steal off of. So one game he decided to steal without a sign. He got a good jump off the pitcher and easily beat the throw to second base. As he shook the dirt off his uniform, Jackson smiled with delight, feeling he had vindicated his judgment to his manager.

Later Weaver took Jackson aside and explained why he hadn't given the steal sign. First, the next batter was Lee May, his best power hitter other than Jackson. When Jackson stole second, first base was left open, so the other team walked May intentionally, taking the bat out of his hands.

Second, the following batter hadn't been strong against that pitcher, so Weaver felt he had to send up a pinch hitter to try to drive in the men on base. That left Weaver without bench strength later in the game when he needed it.

The problem was, Jackson saw only his relationship to the pitcher and catcher. Weaver was watching the whole game.[1]

There are going to be times as parents when you will see the larger picture while your child is focused only on a particular section. If he doesn't trust you, he will make his decision without all of the facts. If he does trust you, he will heed your perspective. Sometimes this advice, especially in the teen-age years could be life-and-death matters. With drugs and alcohol, sexually transmitted diseases such as AIDS, and guns and gangs, your child will face life-and-death choices. He needs to be able to trust your larger perspective.

Someone might say that explanation is more important than trust. If you tell your child to do something, he deserves an explanation, not just a "Trust me." I agree, but sometimes there is no time for explanation.

In the Belgian Congo, the weather was hot and dank. No breath of air stirred; leaves hung from the trees as though they were weighted. In the garden not far from the missionary home a small boy played under a tree. Suddenly, the father called to him: "Philip, obey me instantly—get down on your stomach." The boy reacted at once, and his father continued, "Now crawl toward me fast." The boy again obeyed. After he had come about halfway, the father said, "Now stand up and run to me." The boy reached his father and turned to look back—hanging from the branch under which he had been playing was a fifteen-foot serpent.[2]

> *If they trust you, they will obey. If they don't, they probably won't.*

When there is no time for explanation, all you can rely on is trust. If they trust you, they will obey. If they don't, they probably won't.

• **Trust ensures confidence.**

Your child will look for someone in whom he can confide. Of course, as his parent, you will desire that to be you. A strong trust between you and your child will encourage him to tell you his fears, his dreams, his failures, and his desires. Without trust, he will search out a friend, a schoolteacher, a counselor, or someone else. That person will have the position, intended for you, to implant his wisdom in your child's head that will guide him to make decisions that will shape his entire life.

Strong, overbearing authority does not encourage confidence. People tremble before a judge. To the contrary, all love is often void of rationale, and therefore does not build confidence in the child who wants to hear reality. Consequently, neither authority nor love accomplishes this task—only trust.

Whom Should You Trust?

Does it make a difference *to your child* whom he trusts?

Absolutely! Your child will pick and choose whom he will trust and will respond accordingly. This is illustrated in the following story:

> *Looking through binoculars in the Alps, a group of scientists saw a healthy specimen of a rare plant that they wanted. It was located, however, on a valley floor. Although they had ropes and climbing equipment, the cliffs appeared too steep for anyone of their weight. Just then a young lad with his dog came bounding down the path. They stopped him with this proposition: for a certain amount of money they would tie a strong rope around his waist, lower him to the valley floor, and draw him up again when he had uprooted the plant. He considered a moment, then without a word returned the way he had come. In a few minutes, however, he again appeared, leading by the hand a burly Swiss mountaineer. "All right, gentlemen," he said, "I will get your plant. But my father will hold the rope."*[3]

Does it make a difference *to you* whom your child trusts?

It should! From God's perspective, what is the most fundamental goal of parenting? It is to lead your child into a trusting relationship with the Lord Jesus Christ. Roff Zettersten says, "Therein lies the ultimate objective for the family—to nurture precious souls into God's kingdom."[4] All born of

> *Children look to their parents to find the way to God.*

woman have a need for God. The Lord places it in your heart. Children look to their parents to find the way to God. Parents, therefore, should be the ones who challenge their children to follow Christ all the days of their lives. The most ideal way to do this is to build trust between you and your children. Then teach them, as they grow older and more independent, their need to transfer their trust not to themselves, but to God.

You want to have this position of influence in their lives. Trust ensures that you will.

For the Roman families during the time of Christ, there was no greater honor bestowed upon a family than to have three genera-tions in ruling positions.[5] I would remind you that there is no greater honor bestowed upon a Christian family than to have three genera-tions written in the Book of Life. Make this your goal. Make this your passion. Make this a moun-tain that you would gladly die on. The task these days of directing our offspring toward God is more challenging than ever. Are you up to it? I hope so. Your child's destiny depends upon it.

> *There is no greater honor bestowed upon a Christian family than to have three generations written in the Book of Life.*

Trust-Busters

Practically speaking, all of the examples where children feel their parents are untrustworthy fall under the category of inconsistent living. You as a parent, have to be consistent in your day-to-day activities. The Bible says in Proverbs 20:7, "The righteous man walks in his integrity; his children are blessed after him." A righteous man is blameless. He is consistent. He is a man of integrity. His children are blessed because of this. They can trust him.

A righteous man who is a good parent walks in integrity with a consistent life that he models before his children. Now I realize that you are not perfect. It is not that you must never make a mistake before your children. It is rather that you never make a mistake on purpose. Your child needs to see modeled before him a life motivated and driven toward being holy. D.L. Moody once said, "A holy life will make the deepest impression. Lighthouses blow no horns: they just shine."[6]

Friedrich Nietzsche, who espoused the "God is dead" movement, had this to say, "The greatest hindrance to Christianity are the Chris-tians."[7] You, as a parent, have the ability to demonstrate before your child the riches and blessings found in Christianity, or you can present a hypocrisy from which they will almost surely never recover. It is the difference in presenting a steak on a silver platter that you will almost certainly gobble up, or on a garbage lid, whereby that steak may be juicy and delicious, but you won't touch it because of its presentation. The choice is up to you.

Never Lie to Your Child

If you choose the silver platter presentation, you must lead a blameless life. This starts by never lying to, or in front of, your children. Don't lie! That stands for everything from white lies to cheating a little on your income taxes. Once anyone can find blame, you cease to be blameless.

You can lie to your child in not being consistent in what you have promised. One Father brought his two-year-old little girl in for a yearly check-up. He was not prepared for a two-year-old's conduct in a treatment room. She was nude, frightened, and wanting her mother. Following the examination, the father picked up his daughter off the table. She began to kick and cry at the top of her lungs. This was normal.

> *Once you can find blame, you cease to be blameless.*

As is my custom, I gave the child a balloon. The father said, "Tell him thank you." She only cried louder. The father repeated, "Tell him thank you." She cried even louder. Finally, the father said, "If you don't tell him thank you, you have to give him back the balloon." Then he took the balloon from her and said, "Say thank you." Of course, she did not say thank you. He then handed the balloon back to her, and they left. The father lied to the daughter that day. The father had made a promise and then he didn't carry it through. She challenged the system that day, and she won.

Lying can be found in many forms. Whether it be a promise unfulfilled, a casual statement only partially true (often termed a white lie), or a fairy tale portrayed as reality, it is all lying.

Santas, Easter Bunnies, Fairies, Ghosts, Goblins, and Gremlins

What is our number-one goal in parenting? It is to teach our children to trust Christ. What is the number-one way to do this? It is to first get them to trust us, and then transfer that trust to Christ. What is the number-one way for them not to do this? It is for us, as parents, to be found untrustworthy and hypocritical toward Christianity.

Christmas

Now we must address a very volatile and controversial subject—holidays. Is teaching your children to believe in Santa, the Easter Bunny, and the Tooth Fairy lying to them? You tell me. If I told you, friend, there is a man from the North Pole coming to bring you a gift tonight. It is free, and he just wants to bring it because you have been good. There is another man from Heaven who is bringing you another gift. It is also free, and he just wants to bring it because he loves you. I ask you, as an adult: Can you tell the difference between the reality of these two stories? Probably not. Let me help you further. Let's say the next morning, the package from the man from the North Pole was sitting in your living room. Who are you, as an adult, more apt to believe exists: the man from the North Pole who brought you a gift you can touch and feel and play with, or the man from Heaven whose gift is a concept for you to only think about? If you have trouble distinguishing which is real, how much more so do your children? So I'll ask you again: Is teaching your children to believe in Santa lying to them?

> *Is teaching your children to believe in Santa, the Easter Bunny, and the Tooth Fairy lying to them?*

This is why we must address this issue. I really believe this is the first generation of Americans who have had to deal with this dilemma. Why is it so important now? Because our world is bent on obliterating any reference to God from entering the ears of our children. There used to be a day when children would hear stories of the nativity from the elementary school teachers. They would hear Presidents tell of Christ's birth. Everyone from the schoolhouse to the White House would be proclaiming Christmas as Jesus' birthday. But that is not the case today.

There has been a total reversal on the emphasis of Christmas. Now, the message our children are hearing from the world authorities is that Christmas is all about Santa. To undermine it further, they are saying that there is no God. In fact, you cannot in our public schools even make reference to Jesus having anything to do with Christmas. The focus of this holiday has been completely distorted.

Now with that in mind, how should we as responsible Christians approach this with our children? Let me say first and foremost, I do not want to rob any child of his imagination and creativity. But we must understand that the world we were raised in is not the world in which our children will be raised. In the past, there were not as many dangers attacking the trust in a family, and therefore, it was more acceptable to allow your children to believe in Santa. A parent could balance appropriately the time spent sharing about the birth of Jesus and the coming of Santa. Parents could depend upon the other authorities over that child to keep this balance. But that guarantee is gone. Now our children may hear a balance at home, yet in the world they will certainly hear nothing but Santa. Now, this has a great potential to affect a child's belief system and consequently put their trust in you in jeopardy. Why?

When children reach the age of five or six, they will begin to develop their critical thinking skills. They will question the validity of God, and the validity of Santa. Most of their authorities, except you, are telling them there is no God, only Santa. You are telling them there are both. What confusion this will cause in the child. Now, I am not saying that by letting them believe in Santa you are setting them up for massive distrust in you. What I am saying is to **search out an alternative without lying to your children.** If they can find blame, you cease to be blameless. Why give them one more piece of ammo to fire at you later in life? The choice is yours.

Here is an alternative. Play the game of Santa but make sure that

If you don't proclaim Christ at Christmas, who will?

they know it is just a game. Then stress heavily the birth of Christ at Christmas. You are a Christian. If you don't proclaim Christ at Christmas, who will? Explain that Jesus is not a game we play, but complete reality. That way your child can explore his imagination in the atmosphere of a game, and consequently keep you from lying to him about Santa. Now, of course, this is just one of many alternatives.

My son's family traditionally will act out the nativity scene on Christmas Eve. My granddaughter, Mary Grace, is of course Mary; her "Baby Doll" is Baby Jesus; Jack, my grandson, is Joseph; and the family dog is of course the donkey. My son is the shepherd and my daughter-in-law is the angel. They dress up and create quite a memory. Here is another chance for you to be creative. Just do what is right and what the Lord leads you to do.

I want to end this section on Christmas with something to ponder. On an episode of the popular television show, "Candid Camera," they asked children the question "What is Christmas?" Every child interviewed said something about Santa with the exception of one. This six-year-old boy said, "When Jesus was born." They asked him, "Who is Jesus?" His answer, "One of our Presidents." They then asked him, "If it's Jesus' birthday, why do you get presents?" The little boy said, "Because he is dead and he couldn't get presents." All of these children related Christmas to Santa, except one. He saw Jesus as a dead figure of history. Is there any doubt as to why we have a generation rebelling against the church? They don't even know who Jesus is. This is why I strongly ask you to take seriously this challenge to reserve Christmas as a God-given time to teach your child about Jesus. You will not be disappointed that you did.

Halloween

The following is a story that I retrieved from the Internet from a twelve-year-old boy about his fascination with Wiccans (modern-day witchcraft).

I'd like to say that I think that you are one of the only religions in the world to actually have a clue. Several things come to mind. First: "Do as you will, and in it harm none." is about

*the single [most] thing used by any religious creed that is intelli-
gent. Second: your feelings about magic, especially about harmful
magic, are very intelligent also. Third: Everyone is just so peaceful and down to earth, especially after centuries of hate and mis-
trust; it is just short of amazing. You are one of the only groups in
the world that I consider intelligent and wise enough to actually
handle your problems "maturely." You are all to be commended
for all aspects of your religion.*

Joseph, a 12-year-old non-practicer
(although does sound tempting)

This letter was responded to by the Former High Priest of the
First Church of Wicca, Philadelphia.

*I'm proud of having been Wiccan, and will NEVER put down
what I believed (and still deep down inside, hold as true in many
respects) . . . Young gentleman, you give us all hope for the future.
Not just Wiccans, but all mankind. If all young people could be
as open minded, we could all sleep easy at night.*

Bright Blessings [His Wiccan name]

*P.S. May WHATEVER God(s) or Goddess(es) there be, bless
your young heart.*

Does this scare you? These are the thoughts of a twelve-year-
old. They should scare you. The evil influences pulling at our children
today are astounding. Everything from psychic hotlines to Dungeons
and Dragons are battling for the minds of the youth. Satan makes his
tricks so deceiving, yet so appealing. "Trick or treat" is NOT WHAT
IT USED TO BE!!

If there is ever a day when Christians need to break with the conformity of the world, it is at Halloween.

I don't care how you cut
it, Halloween is Satan's holiday. If
there is ever a day when Christians need to break with the conformity of the world, it is at Halloween. This holiday, while dis-
guised with little boys and girls
dressed as ghosts and devils, has a demonic overcast that reverberates

around the world. Horrific crimes and brutal sacrifices are committed this night in the name of Satan. Why would you want to let your children know by trick-or-treating that Halloween is not only a day you approve of, but one that deserves celebration?

Our children are being hit with these images year-round. Video games and cartoons are replete with demonic characters and forces. Violence seems to be the theme. All of these network themselves together and use Halloween as their climax.

Now, I can hear some of you saying, "But what is wrong with dressing my child up as a cartoon character and taking him through the neighborhood and letting him do 'trick or treat'?" Absolutely nothing. But!!!—you must accept the fact that you are giving your approval to your child of the secular way to celebrate this day attributed solely to Satan. How about an alternative?

I would like to challenge Christians to use Halloween as a day to teach their children the difference between the secular and the holy. Romans 12:2 could be your theme for the day: "Do not be conformed to this world, but be transformed by the renewing of your mind, that you may prove what is that good and acceptable and perfect will of God." If your child cannot learn this at Halloween, when do you expect him to?

Make it fun!! I don't want any child to miss out on fun. Many churches plan Halloween alternatives where children can dress up as Bible characters and meet at the church to play games. I think that is a wonderful idea, and if your church does not do that, perhaps you can be the one to implement it. The key is nonconformity. On Halloween, we typically have a fun night out with my son's family. We will go to a special dinner and then follow with a fun activity for the whole family. We let them dress up in fun costumes, not scary ones, and just have a family night out on the town. I can truly say the grandchildren do not miss out on any fun! It is letting them in on the fact that Christians cannot do everything of which the world approves. Who knows how valuable these lessons will be?

Easter Bunnies and Tooth Fairies

The principles discussed about Christmas apply here too. A lie is still a lie. If you want to play the game, make sure they know that it is just a game. After all, the sooner they learn the tooth fairy is a game, the sooner they will realize that they will get more money giving the tooth to Grandma, instead of Mommy. Make certain they know that a fairy tale is a fairy tale.

> *Make certain they know that a fairy tale is a fairy tale.*

I don't think the Easter bunny needs to be even a game that is played. Sure, it is fine to color eggs and have egg hunts, but your child's mind will be stretched enough if you can convey the resurrection of the Lord to them. I find it amazing what most children remember. When a child thinks of Christmas, Santa is the first thing that pops in his head. When a child thinks of Easter, a bunny rabbit is hopping. This ought not be!

In Summary

The major trust-busters on the parents' part are inconsistencies within their live, like what one father said to his son: "I told you a million times. Stop exaggerating!" Remember what I have said—if they can find blame, you cease to be blameless.

Trust-Builders

What are some things you can do as a parent that will help you build trust between you and your child? Remember this is something to be earned. You must work at it. Here are just a few suggestions.

• **Shape up.**

We have already addressed this one, but it is worth repeating. Model before your children a consistent character that is trustworthy. Allow them to get to know the real you.

If you want them to be men or women of prayer, let them see you pray. If you want them to read their Bible, let them see you read your own. If you want them to give, make sure you are giving yourself. They are watching, and they will imitate. Allow them to observe your faith in action.

This shows them that you are not double-minded. You practice what you preach. You are so confident in the advice you give them that you heed that advice in your own life. This builds trust consistently.

• **Listen up.**

The Greek writer Zeno once said, "We have two ears but only one mouth so that we may hear more and speak less."[8] In James 1:19, James gives parents some excellent advice: "Be swift to hear, slow to speak, and slow to wrath."

How does listening more build trust? First of all, it enables you to learn about your child. When you are listening, he will share those things that matter most. He will confide in you. You can start this at a very young age. Let me show you how.

Don't miss the golden opportunity of sitting on the side of the bed each night with your child. Why is it children don't want to go to bed at night? Perhaps they are afraid they'll miss something. There is somewhat of a ritual in each household at bedtime. We notice there are goodnight kisses for mom, dad, brother, sister, and even the dog. After that, the usual trip to the bathroom is followed by a drink of water. Then, the cycle starts over again and again and again.

I heard about one child who repeatedly asked his mommy for a drink of water. Knowing that the child had an adequate supply of hydration, she insisted that the child stop asking and go to sleep. The child questioned again, "Can I have some more water?" Mommy replied, "No, and if I have to come up there, I'm going to wear you out!" The child thought and then responded, "Mommy, when you come up here to wear me out, will you bring me a glass of water?"

This is the best time for your child to talk. He knows as long as you are there with him, he doesn't have to go to sleep. Just simply ask him what he did today, and then listen to what he has to say. In this given setting, he will be happy to tell you most everything that happened in his day. Sometimes, particularly when he starts to school, he may tell you a dirty joke. You may want to correct the child by saying, "We don't say things like that. It is not nice." But this is not a time for punishment or scolding. It's an opportunity for you to listen and ponder these things in your heart. Even though you are tired and need or want to do other things, don't hurry this special time. It will be gone before you know it.

When your child is older and he becomes more hesitant to talk, or you notice a change for the worse in friends, grades, or attitudes, you need to be suspicious that something is going wrong in his life. It may be drugs, alcohol, sex, or any number of things, but you have been listening to your child all these years. Now you begin to notice a change. You don't have to wait until you receive a surprise phone call at 2:00 a.m. from protective services, telling you that they have your son down at the police headquarters. Don't miss those early opportunities to listen to your child and to know your child. Those moments create happy memories.

By truly listening to your child, especially when he grows older, it shows him that you respect what he has to say. This is a quality he needs to see before he trusts you. This is a way for your child to know that you really care about him. Not that you just tell him that you love him, but you care to know how he is really doing. Your child will pick up on this, and it will matter.

• **Lighten up.**

As your child grows older, he will seek to be more independent. Dennis the Menace told his mom, "I'm tired of you treating me like a baby. Have you noticed how big I'm getting?" His mother replied, "Maybe you're right. You can start by hanging up your clothes, picking up your toys, keeping your room clean, washing your hands without being told, taking out the garbage, feeding Ruff. . . ." "Wait Mom," interrupts Dennis, "if I do all that stuff, you and Dad won't have anything to do." Dennis walks away mumbling, "Boy—you gotta be careful what you say around here!"

It is natural for a growing child to want to be independent. There is nothing wrong with that in and of itself. However, it is often handled incorrectly on both ends. This is usually a time when trust is broken between a parent and a child for a number of reasons. What we want to establish are some ways to maintain that trust, and actually benefit from it, during this often challenging and difficult period.

For some unexplainable reason, people want independence. It has to come from our depraved nature because it is void of rationale. For instance, men will not ask for directions when they are clearly lost. They have to figure it out for themselves. It makes no sense, but it happens. There is a pervading, "I'll do it myself" philosophy that encompasses all of mankind.

On November 20, 1988, the *Los Angeles Times* reported:

> *A screaming woman, trapped in a car dangling from a freeway transition road in East Los Angeles, was rescued Saturday morning. The 19-year-old woman apparently fell asleep behind the wheel about 12:15 a.m. The car, which plunged through a guard rail, was left dangling by its left rear wheel. A half dozen passing motorists stopped, grabbed some ropes from one of their vehicles, tied the ropes to the back of the woman's car, and hung on until the fire units arrived. A ladder was extended from below to help stabilize the car while firefighters tied the vehicle to tow trucks with cables and chains.*
>
> *"Every time we would move the car," said one of the rescuers, "she'd yell and scream. She was in pain."*
>
> *It took almost 2½ hours for the passers-by, CHP officers, tow truck drivers, and firefighters—about 25 people in all—to secure the car and pull the woman to safety.*
>
> *"It was kinda funny," L.A. County Fire Capt. Ross Marshall recalled later. "She kept saying, 'I'll do it myself.'"*[9]

So independence is a given, but how should you handle it? The first thing that must be done is for **everyone to have a complete understanding of the rules.** Now as the child matures those rules will become fewer and fewer and his responsibilities will become more and more. Make sure that everyone is in agreement as to what the rules are.

The next step is to **say yes as often as you can.** When your older child comes to you and asks if he can do something, an affirmative answer gives him confidence. It is confidence in himself that he made a good choice, and confidence in you that you approve of his thinking. This builds his trust in you.

Part of independence is **privacy.** As children grow older, they will tend to want to have their own space. This should be respected by the parents. In addition, let there be an understanding that privacy is a privilege of trust. If a child does something to break that trust, then privacy is no longer his right. This will keep your child thinking and trying to maintain that trust.

> *Let your child reap the natural consequences to his mistakes.*

The older the child becomes, **the parents' role as the punisher decreases.** Now, God has set this world up with penalties for our wrongdoings, so parents can breathe a sigh of relief. Let your child reap the natural consequences of his mistakes. You do not need to come behind him and always double his penalty. At the same time, you don't want to always be bailing him out. For instance, when your child turns sixteen, he may get a speeding ticket. Let him get an extra job to pay off the speeding ticket as well as the difference in his increased insurance rates because of the infraction. Your teenager will increase in his understanding that independence carries with it a great deal of responsibility.

Your child will reach a point when he realizes that his freedom is handcuffed to a great deal of responsibility. This is a great time for you as the parent to teach your child his individual responsibility before Almighty God. Romans 14:12 says, "So then each of us shall give account of himself to God." Your child needs to understand that. Daniel Webster, a famous politician and one of the greatest orators of American history, said, "The most important thought I ever had was my individual responsibility to God."[10]

Now these are just a few suggestions. The changing of the guard, so to speak, is difficult. Cutting the apron strings is tough. But it is worth it. The noblest of all forms of government is self-government, but it is the most difficult to obtain. Make it a gradual process. As children deserve more independence, give it lovingly. Encourage them. Don't be swift to take it back. They will not be perfect at their new freedom. Give them a second and third chance if they genuinely are sorry. After all, how many chances has God given you as His child?

A good example of a father giving his son another chance occurs in the following story. Dennis Miller (not the comedian) writes,

Out of parental concern and a desire to teach our young son responsibility, we require him to phone home when he arrives at his friend's house a few blocks away. He began to forget, however, as he grew more confident in his ability to get there without disaster befalling him.

The first time he forgot, I called to be sure he had arrived. We told him the next time it happened, he would have to come home. A few days later, however, the telephone again lay silent, and I knew if he was going to learn, he would have to be punished. But I did not want to punish him! I went to the telephone, regretting that his great time would have to be spoiled by his lack of contact with his father.

As I dialed, I prayed for wisdom. "Treat him like I treat you," the Lord seemed to say. With that, as the telephone rang one time, I hung up. A few seconds later the phone rang, and it was my son. "I'm here, Dad!"

"What took you so long to call?" I asked.

"We started playing and I forgot. But Dad, I heard the phone ring once, and I remembered."

"I'm glad you remembered," I said. "Have fun."[11]

When God punishes us, He does it in such a way that we can still trust Him. Go and do likewise with your children. More techniques are coming in the next chapters.

Putting It All Together

Corrie ten Boom was a remarkable woman. She experienced first-hand the Nazi concentration camps and lived to tell about it. Her crime: She was German and she loved all people, including Jews. The depth of this woman is astounding. She claims two sources for her strength: first, the omnipotent and omniscient Lord Jesus Christ, and second, her father. I want to center in a moment on the latter. She had a profound respect and trust in her father. She would listen at his feet as he shared his wisdom. She would just soak it up in her heart. They had the type of parent/child relationship that this chapter is all about. See if you can see the benefits in a child's trusting her father, which are shown in this little story written by Corrie in her bestseller, *The Hiding Place.*

> *Once—I must have been ten or eleven—I asked Father about a poem we had read at school the winter before. One line had described "a young man whose face was not shadowed by sexsin." I had been far too shy to ask the teacher what it meant, and Mama had blushed scarlet when I consulted her. In those days just after the turn of the century sex was never discussed, even at home.*
>
> *So the line had stuck in my head. "Sex," I was pretty sure, meant whether you were a boy or a girl, and "sin" made Tante Jans very angry, but what the two together meant I could not imagine. And so, seated next to Father in the train compartment, I suddenly asked, "Father, what is sexsin?"*
>
> *He turned to look at me, as he always did when answering a question, but to my surprise he said nothing. At last he stood up, lifted his traveling case from the rack over our heads, and set it on the floor.*
>
> *"Will you carry it off the train, Corrie?" he said.*
>
> *I stood up and tugged at it. It was crammed with the watches and spare parts he had purchased that morning.*
>
> *"It's too heavy," I said.*
>
> *"Yes," he said. "And it would be a pretty poor father who would ask his little girl to carry such a load. It's the same way, Corrie, with knowledge. Some knowledge is too heavy for children. When you are older and stronger you can bear it. For now you must trust me to carry it for you." And I was satisfied. More than satisfied—wonderfully at peace. There were answers to this and all my hard questions—for now I was content to leave them in my father's keeping.*[12]

Can Your Kids Trust You?

Corrie ten Boom trusted her father. She trusted him to the point of being more than satisfied letting him make decisions that would drastically affect her life. But why? Why did she trust him so? He led a blameless life. Her father represented Christ in all that he did. He also spent hours at her bedside teaching her about the Lord. When her father was gone, guess whom she turned to? You got it; the Lord became her invaluable source of strength that enabled her to survive her imprisonment. Then she recognized her individual responsibility before God to share her story with the world.

Chapter 6

To Discipline or
Not to Discipline?
That Isn't a Question!

Even a child is known by his deeds.
Whether what he does is pure and right.

PROVERBS 20:11

To Discipline or Not to Discipline? That Isn't a Question!

D iscipline is to love, authority, and trust, what ink is to a pen. That is, when implementing love, authority, and trust, you are incorporating discipline. To use our painting scenario, each time you pick up a paintbrush, you are dipping it in the paint of discipline.

Paints come in many textures and mixtures, as well as many colors. So does discipline. This is why training a child is not a system, it is an art form. You will take your methods and your styles and match them with your unique child. Some days you will paint big broad specialty colors and use the "love" brush to do it. Other days the primary basic colors will be painted with the "authority" brush to establish basic guidelines for your home. Sometimes a thin layer of highlight colors will be used to build trust at a time when it seems to be broken. No matter which brush and what style of paint you use, they will all take part in training your child.

Discipline is used to combat your child's inbred nature to do wrong. Now some people would say that children are born perfect; however, I think just the opposite. The Bible teaches that "all have sinned and fallen short of the glory of God" (Romans 3:23). It seems as though the moment they exit the womb they begin to partake of the sinful nature of their ancestor, Adam. One four-year-old boy was looking at his new sister, who was screaming at the top of her lungs. He said to his mother, "Has she just come from heaven?" His mother answered, "Why, yes." The son responded, "Well, it's no wonder they threw her out."

It seems the moment children are born the behavioral problems begin. One lady was frantically searching for a card in a gift shop. The clerk sensed her frustration and asked, "May I help you?" She replied, "I'm looking for a card for a mother of newborn triplets." The clerk responded, "How about a sympathy card?"

As children grow, so does their ability to misbehave. Two boys were trying to outdo each other. The first said, "My uncle is a doctor. I can be sick for nothing." The second youngster said, "Big deal! My uncle is a preacher. I can be good for nothing."

Before you know it, it is time to send that bundle of behaviors to school to let others share in your confusion. One teacher notified her student, "That's the fifth time I've had to punish you this week. What have you got to say for yourself?" "Thank goodness it's Friday!"

Then your child will feebly try to convince you that it is the school with the problems. One child told his mother, "My teacher punished me for something I didn't do." "What was that?" questioned his mom. "My homework."

Another little boy came home and told his dad, "There is a small PTA meeting today and you gotta go." His dad, puzzled, asked, "If it's so small, why do I have to go?" The boy replied, "It's between you, me, and the principal."

You can always tell the people who don't have children. They are the ones who think the summer went by so fast.

It doesn't take long for parents to realize their child is bent to misbehave. The Bible says in Proverbs 20:11, "Even a child is known by his deeds, whether what he does is pure and right." Your job as a parent is to train your child in the way of purity and righteousness. Discipline is the parent's tool for charting the new course. One

> *God's children are much like earthly children—they are prone to misbehave.*

man said, "The behavior of some children suggests that their parents embarked on the sea of matrimony without a paddle."[1]

We have tried to establish throughout this book principles that are used by God himself. In discussing discipline, we again want to turn to see how Father God enforces His standards and encourages the obedience of His children. God's children are much like earthly children—they are prone to misbehave.

God's Discipline

God is a God of love. The Bible says in 1 John 4:8b, "God is love." God is a God of authority. In Romans 13:1, it says, "For there is no authority except from God, and the authorities that exist are appointed by God." Not only is God a God of love and a God of authority, but He is also a God of trust. Psalm 4:5b declares, "Put your trust in the LORD." Why? Look at Psalm 34:22, "The LORD redeems the soul of His servants, and none of those who trust in Him shall be condemned."

So there you have it: God is a God of love, authority, and trust. All three elements are perfectly in balance. Yet, His children were and are disobedient. He was the perfect parent, but despite that, His children misbehaved. Why? They were individuals with a depraved choice to do what was right in their own eyes. Your child is the same way. No matter how well you establish your love, authority, and trust, you will still find yourself battling the fallen nature of your child.

What did God do when His children misbehaved? He disciplined them. It was because He had the three perfectly in balance that He was forced to discipline them when they needed it. Deuteronomy 8:5 tells us, "You should know in your heart that as a man chastens his son, so the LORD your God chastens you." Judges 13:1 says, "Again the children of Israel did evil in the sight of the LORD, and the LORD delivered them into the hand of the Philistines for forty years." You may be thinking, "Forty years is a pretty harsh penalty. I thought He was a God of love." He is. He loved them enough to discipline them properly. He knew what it would take to get their attention.

Some parents don't discipline their children because they are afraid their children will quit loving them. That is nonsense; discipline demonstrates to your child that you do indeed love them. Proverbs 3:11-12 explains, "My son, do not despise the chastening of the *Discipline your children because it is right, and it is what God says to do.* LORD, nor detest His correction; for whom the LORD loves He corrects, just as a father the son in whom he delights." Even Job said, "Happy is the man whom God corrects; therefore do not despise the chastening of the Almighty" (5:17).

God has set discipline as the method and mode to drive disobedience out of man. Don't discipline because I say to. Don't even discipline because you think you should. Discipline your children because it is right, and it is what God says to do.

How Do I Discipline?

Several years ago, I was approached by a doctor from Vanderbilt University who desired to conduct a study in my office. He wanted to interview the patients before I had the opportunity to see them. I consented to do this only because I knew the doctor so well. This doctor would go into the treatment room and question the patients as to the real nature of their visit that day to the office. Surprisingly, he found that seventy percent of the patients that came in were worried about child behavior. The discipline of their children was the essential reason for their visit. Of course, they came under the disguise of sore throats, vomiting, and headaches, but their underlying concern was child behavior or child discipline. As a result of that study I redirected my practice to meet these needs.

Most experts on child discipline would agree that there are four basic styles of parenting as it relates to discipline. Often the factor that determines a parent's proclivity toward one particular style is from a reaction to the style in which they were raised. The four styles are Authoritarian, Indifferent, Permissive, and Authoritative.

Authoritarian (My Way, or the Highway)

Authoritarian is characterized as tough, rigid, toe-the-line, no bargaining or explaining by the child to the parent, firmness with children, strict authority over the child. This style often conveys to the child strong authority with little love and affection. This is also known as the Victorian way of rearing children. It was very popular in the 1930s to the 1950s and is responsible for the outbreak of many other alternatives to parenting.

**Permissiveness
(Your Wish Is My Command)**

This philosophy, promoted by Dr. Spock, has produced a generation of undisciplined, rebellious teen-agers. Permissiveness is characterized as few do's and don'ts,

Permissiveness has produced a generation of undisciplined, rebellious teen-agers.

total freedom for the child, easy, laid back, everything will be okay, let the child do "his thing," let him express himself freely and totally in his own way. It's a rather "eat, drink, and be merry" type of discipline. Often the parent is able to express love to the child but fails to maintain any authority in the home.

Indifference (I Couldn't Care Less)

Indifference is a third style of parenting. These parents seem from an outsider's point of view not to care about their children. The lack of authority is not because the parent thinks it is best, but rather that the parent doesn't care to take the time to do anything about it. This style is perhaps the most devastating because the child is raised without rules, combined with almost no love and affection.

Authoritative (I Correct You Because I Love You)

Finally, the style I want you to work hard to achieve is authoritative. Don't get this confused with authoritarian. The authoritative philosophy is more of a balanced, central, middle-of-the-road style. It seeks to show affectionate love to the child in a structured environment with firm authority. Most parents either fall into this category or wish they were in it. The largest number of well-adjusted, achieving children are found to have had this form of discipline. Strive to obtain this style.

While these are called discipline styles, they do not give us much information about how each style would implement discipline. I think these refer more to parenting styles than they do disciplining styles. You see, the parenting style advocated in this book is one where standards are firmly set in an atmosphere of love and authority. These balanced together will work toward the goal of a solid trusting relationship between the parent and the child. This is a modified authoritative style of parenting. But how is discipline achieved in this setting?

Mere softness is not enough. In railway trains there is a mechanism to prevent one rail car from hitting another. At the outer surface of this contraption, where the cars are more apt to hit, there is a soft, spongy covering. Within this, at the very center, is a spring. It is strong but yielding, yielding but strong.[2] That is what is needed in this style of parenting—strong discipline with a soft covering of love. Abraham

Lincoln possessed a character like this. He was once described as a man of "velvet steel." He was soft, tender, and gentle as velvet, yet as unbending, secure, and strong as steel. Become parents like velvet steel.

It is amazing to me that those in leadership positions across America do not turn to discipline as a means of correcting the rebellious youth. The substitutes they promote in place of discipline are amazing. You wonder how in the world they reached their powerful positions flaunting these irrational ideas.

I am reminded of one teen-ager who was out of control. Many times, he would slam his hand through the wall when he got mad and was destroying his parents' house. He was informed that he could not come back to school because of his disruptive behavior and failure to complete his assignments. There was absolutely no discipline in his family.

The teen-ager was referred to a psychologist who outlined a program for him, called behavioral modification. The following is the actual prescription of what this licensed psychologist thought would do the trick:

1. Preferential seating away from as much auditory and visual stimuli as possible.
2. Give only one instruction at a time.
3. Reduce the competitive edge.
4. Teach note-taking skills.
5. Use time out for inappropriate behavior such as interrupting or being aggressive or resistant.
   - If he continues to exhibit significant problems after these behavior modifications have been attempted for a reasonable amount of time, medical intervention should be considered.

Do you think this teen-ager improved? Of course not. We have a dominant pool of professionals who are treating misbehavior as a disease. They are treating the child as a victim of his hormones. They are advocating drugs as the only answer.

I am here to say—hogwash!!! What this boy needed was some good, old-fashioned discipline. You have been gracious enough to give me your time to hear practical advice on parenting. You will not find a new hidden technique in this book. I am trying to restore the techniques that used to produce hardworking, normal, happy adults. It is God's way, not mine. I am getting ready to flood you with techniques that work. They are tried and they are proven.

Three Goals for Discipline

There are three goals that proper discipline will achieve. Discipline will first of all provide a penalty for disobedience. Second, it will be instrumental in training and teaching the child proper conduct. And finally, it will nurture a life of self-discipline that will be invaluable for the child's success. Let's look at these in more detail.

1. A Penalty for Disobedience

If we want our children to respect the law when they are older, we must put the fear of punishment in them when they are young.

Proverbs 15:10 says, "Stern discipline awaits him who leaves the path" (NIV). Many people today have picked up the idea that punishing a child breaks his spirit. Therefore, they adopt alternate methods such as behavioral modification, which was discussed above. Once again we are protecting the guilty. These same people are more concerned with privileges for the prisoners than for justice to be done. There must be a penalty for wrongdoing.

While punishment should never be used as revenge, it is an effective means of discipline. God says stern discipline, or harsh discipline, awaits the disobedient who leaves the correct path. Ruth Alexander says, "Punishment must be used to instill fear of the consequences of criminal acts, in order to protect the law-abiding."[3] If we want our children to respect the law when they are older, we must put the fear of punishment in them when they are young.

As for the idea that punishment will break their spirit, the Bible teaches otherwise. Punishment is used to drive them back to the correct path. Discipline is basic, but sometimes it can be quite painful to both the parent and the child. An easy road, void of any pain, does not dictate a successful life. In fact, oftentimes the more difficult the road, the better the person. Someone has made the observation, "The sturdiest tree is not found in the shelter of the forest, but high upon some rocky crag, where its daily battle with the elements shapes it into a thing of beauty."[4]

> *"Child training is merely knowing which end of your child to pat . . . and when."*

The key is mixing authority in with love and trust. Punishment is harmful when the child does not have the counterbalance of love to build him up. Jan Marshall said, "You can never go wrong by giving a youngster lots of love and kisses mixed with discipline. Child training is merely knowing which end of your child to pat . . . and when."[5]

2. Teaching Proper Conduct

I want us to think about two verses. The first is Proverbs 6:23, "For these commands are a lamp, this teaching is a light, and the corrections of discipline are the way to life" (NIV). The second verse is Psalms 94:12, "Blessed is the man you discipline, O LORD, the man you teach from your law" (NIV). I see three elements in these verses: commands, teaching, and discipline. These two verses describe their relationship to each other.

Think of walking down a dark path with nothing but an oil lamp. You have never walked down this path so everything is a new experience. As you walk, the light shines on new areas and teaches you about the surroundings of your travel. If you get off the path, the light still exposes your surroundings and you learn more of what is there.

Now let's bring this together with these two verses. The rules of your home simply contain the oil that will teach the child. They allow the child to operate within reason. As the child walks, he will learn; his path is illuminated by the light. The choice to stay on the path is left to the child. No matter whether he chooses to stay or to leave, in either case, he will learn. However, getting off the path may lead to destruction. This is where discipline comes in. Discipline will drive the child back on the right path, the way to life.

So that is the relationship to rules, teaching, and discipline. Rules do not teach; they simply enable the child to learn. Teaching comes by experiencing life; it can be good or bad. Discipline encourages those lessons to be good. Therefore, discipline teaches proper conduct.

3. Promote Self-Discipline

Robert L. Garner wrote in the *Kiwanis Magazine*,

Self-discipline is the ultimate test of the worth of the free man or woman. It does not rest on fear of punishment, nor on the dictates of superior authority, nor on the willingness to go along and be a good member of the team. It is a quality that evolves as the individual develops certain standards of conduct, which for him have sufficient value that to uphold them he will endure whatever comes.[6]

Do you have a goal for your parenting? If not, you should. If you need one, here it is: that your child develop self-discipline. This is the final stage of discipline. It is the point where an individual becomes his own authority and operates properly underneath it. It is the result of parenting that taught a young child the importance of obedience and enforced it with discipline.

A life walking in obedience will experience far fewer troubles. Proverbs 13:18 says, "Poverty and shame will come to him who disdains correction, but he who regards a rebuke will be honored." He will be honored with the way to life. They not only honor themselves, but also their parents, and hopefully, one day, honor God.

In Summary

The three purposes of discipline are:
1. Penalizing Disobedience
2. Teaching Proper Conduct
3. Promoting Self-Discipline

Your Child is Your Priority

In the Nashville *Tennessean* on Thursday, September 8, 1983, an article appeared entitled "Discipline Must Be Enforced." Here are some of the excerpts from that article:

> *All parents have to discipline their children from time to time, and that's particularly difficult when both parents work. "My kids slide by," said the mother of two girls, eleven and thirteen years old. "I don't want to nag them so I close the doors to their messy rooms and close my eyes when they don't fold their clothes. My youngest has the table manners of an untrained monkey. I let things slide because I just don't have the energy. I still lower the boom if they defy me, but I can't keep up with the daily discipline that kids seem to need. I can't punish them because I can't enforce the punishment. They both are out of hand—it is clear they both need discipline."[7]*

This poor mother knows that her children need discipline, yet she is unwilling to relinquish enough of her personal life to provide it. Something is wrong when your children are not a priority. They are your chief responsibility, and their welfare should come first. This seems to be common sense, but despite this fact, children surprisingly often fail to reach the priority list of their parents.

A cartoon depicted a child standing in the doorway as his parents were getting ready to leave the house. The child disappointedly looked up and said, "PTA, Scouts, church meetings—but when are you going to stay home with me?" Your child is your most important business.

I received a call at the office one day from a mother who informed me that her child had just had a seizure. I told her to bring the child in immediately. She responded, "I am at work right now, and I can't bring him in before tomorrow." This is not right. Your child is your most important business.

I'll never forget a little four-year-old boy waiting for me in treatment room number two. This little fellow looked up in my eyes and asked me, "Why doesn't my mom make me mind and spank me occasionally?" I looked at the mother and she just dropped her head. She knew that she had not given the proper time to her child, but she was surprised that her child was aware of it as well. Please remember, your child is your most important business.

To Discipline or Not to Discipline? That Isn't a Question!

There was another child I recall who was very perceptive to priorities. Just about every week this little first grader would come into the office with a laceration. I thought at first that he just played hard, but the child kept coming in over and over and over—so I got suspicious. There was no evidence of child abuse, yet the lacerations continued. One day I asked the child how he was getting all of these cuts. He shocked me with his answer. He said, "If mother will quit work, I'll quit doing this to myself." This child would come home an hour and a half before her. He would purposefully cut himself to try to get his mother's attention. He was willing to go through this pain so his mother would come home early from work. His mother had no idea. The mother rearranged her schedule to be at home when the child arrived. They did not return with any more cuts. Here is a mother who has finally learned that her child is her most important business.

Folks, your children need you. Many parents today are handing out almost all their responsibilities to others. Parents end up being largely suppliers of food, clothing, and a taxi service. Your children must be your ultimate priority. You must give the time to train them and not leave them to themselves. The Bible says in Proverbs 29:15: "The rod and rebuke give wisdom, but a child left to himself brings shame to his mother."

> ## "The first step in disciplining a child is to discipline oneself."

Marcelene Cox stated in *Ladies Home Journal*, "The first step in disciplining a child is to discipline oneself."[8] We have demanded neither respect nor responsible behavior from our children because we are too busy with our own lives. Therefore, I don't think it should be surprising that some of our children are now demonstrating the absence of these qualities.

For example, a six-year-old child was in the hospital, having broken her arm, and was lying on her back in traction. Each day as I made my usual hospital rounds, I observed an unbelievable behavior. The child was repeatedly spitting in her mother's face. I asked the mother what she was going to do about it. Her reply was, "I'll have to talk with her when I get her home." That was code for: "I don't care enough to discipline her now." I don't think I would have postponed needed discipline that long.

Parents, you have a responsibility to raise your children in a way that far surpasses anything else in your life. Children are perishing, in many cases, because parents are not doing their job. Proverbs 5:23 says, "He shall die for lack of discipline, led astray by his own great folly" (NIV).

> *A boy in Aesop's time stole a horn-book, and took it to his mother. She praised him for it. From that time he pursued a course of crime till he was detected, and sentenced to execution. At the last he called his mother to him and bit off her ear. The crowd upbraided him for his unnatural cruelty. He replied, "It is she who is the cause of my ruin; for if, when I stole my school-fellow's horn-book, and brought it to her, she had given me a sound flogging, I should never have so grown in wickedness as to come to this untimely end."[9]*

"Discipline your son, for in that there is hope; do not be a willing party to his death."—Proverbs 19:18 (NIV).

The Myth That Love Conquers All

In my practice I recall vividly a mother who had adopted two babies two years apart. During those developing years, I was never allowed to examine the children until after asking the mother to step aside. Each time I entered the treatment room, she was hugging, loving, kissing, and hovering over the children so that I could not examine them. Even as the children were in grade school and high school this type of behavior continued from the mother. Frequently, I discussed discipline of the children with her and the reply was always, "I love them too much to discipline them." She never punished or corrected them.

At age seventeen, her daughter was seated on the examining table with the mother hugging, kissing, and telling her how much she loved her, when I opened the door and entered the room. Immediately, the daughter leaned back and almost slapped the mother to the floor. After I had regained my composure, I asked the mother what she intended to do. Her reply was, "Just love her."

Some parents never get it. You would think that slap would have sent a wake-up call to her, but it didn't. Some parents can never bring themselves to notice that their children have messed up. I heard about one set of parents who were bragging about their children to some friends. "We are very proud of our boy in school. He has been president of the Sophomore Class for three years."

A father was overheard telling another, "My child has been in college two terms: President Reagan and President Bush." A large number of parents today believe that total love makes discipline obsolete. There are others who believe in discipline, but fail to implement it properly for fear that they will jeopardize that love.

A parent may love a child too much to feed him properly, or love a child too much to develop proper sleeping habits for him. These are the two most common problems in early childhood. I will discuss some healthful techniques in the chapters to come.

Discipline can be quite painful for both the parent and the child. Words that hurt may be exchanged in the heat of battle. When the fire settles and the routines begin again, remember that your children are better off because you disciplined. Proverbs 13:24: "He who spares his rod hates his son, but he who loves him disciplines him promptly."

> *"He who spares his rod hates his son, but he who loves him disciplines him promptly."*

Do not withhold discipline for the sake of love. The Bible says in Proverbs 23:13: "Do not withhold discipline from a child; if you punish him with the rod, he will not die" (NIV). Someone has well said, "The prevalence of juvenile delinquency is proving that some parents are not getting at the SEAT of the problem."[10] While disciplining a child is painful, it is nothing compared to weeping over a spoiled youth.[11] In a day when character runs very thin, "Many parents are finding that a pat on the back helps redevelop character in children . . . if given often, early, and low enough."[12]

But I Don't Know How to Discipline

Many of you are probably thinking, "I know I need to discipline but how?" I think it is important to spend some time to establish the need to discipline, because so many don't feel it is necessary. Hopefully, you see the importance of prioritizing your schedule to meet the needs of your children, especially when it comes to discipline.

The next two chapters are going to be replete with practical techniques to discipline and train your children. There are many techniques out there that work and many that do not. This often gets parents very confused. One mother of a two-year-old asked an expert on children, "If one of my children is a pain and the other is a pill, shouldn't they cancel each other out?" Another mother asked, "If children should be seen and not heard, does that mean they should be bound and gagged?"

On a recent survey, forty-seven percent of parents said that the process of rearing children had been more difficult than they had imagined. Often it is because parents don't know which methods work. They lack the confidence to enforce any of them well. One mother asked a very puzzling question, "Why do we spend the first two years teaching our kids to walk and talk and the next sixteen telling them to shut up and sit down?"

What makes the next two chapters so reliable? Mark Twain said, "Good judgment comes from experience. Experience comes from bad judgment."[13] These techniques are the byproduct of over forty years of experience and seeing tens of thousands of children raised into adulthood. These are methods that work. They have been tried and proven over and over and over again. I hope this will give you the faith to implement these discipline techniques with confidence.

I want to close this chapter with a few quotations from wise men speaking the truth concerning children.

*Let a pig and a boy have everything they want,
and you'll get a good pig and a bad boy.*[14]

*Everything nowadays is controlled by switches—
except children.*[15]

To Discipline or Not to Discipline? That Isn't a Question!

It isn't what you know that counts;
it's what you think of in time.

The cost of obedience is nothing compared with
the cost of disobedience.[16]

What has been done in the childhood years has a lot to do
with the solving of problems in the teen years.
Crime is not corrected in the electric chair,
but in the high chair.[17]

Correct your son, and he will give you rest;
Yes, he will give you delight to your soul. —*Proverbs 29:17*

Chapter 7

Tools for Training: From Rods to Rewards

Now no chastening seems to be joyful for the present, but painful; nevertheless, afterward it yields the peaceable fruit of righteousness to those who have been trained by it.

HEBREWS 12:11

O nce again, I want to allow my younger son to share a story that taught him a great lesson and I hope will teach us a great lesson concerning the discipline of our children.

A few years ago, I was traveling in the land of Israel to experience the world as Jesus saw it. My wife and I decided to go with our group on a desert safari through the Judean Wilderness. Now my Western mind pondered a nice drive through the countryside in a comfortable air-conditioned Jeep Cherokee. Well, I was wrong. Instead, a diesel truck pulled up with an open-air trailer hooked to the back. Yes—we rode in the trailer, about thirty of us in all.

I want to give you a little tourism advice in case you decide to go to Israel. There are NO roads on the Judean Wilderness Desert Safari. Hear me, NO roads!! This really sat well with my Type B personality.

I mistakenly got on the end seat, second row from the back. This was error number two. Error number one was going on the Judean Wilderness Desert Safari. The next thing I knew we were driving down dried-up river beds, over rocky hills, and down into craggy, jagged valleys. Needless to say, it was a rough ride. It felt as though we were driving over two-foot speed bumps at thirty miles per hour.

The paths we traveled on were no wider than the truck. Did you hear me? I mean there was NO side. A median was non-existent. It was definitely one way. If the vehicle was six feet wide, the path in some places was no more than six feet six inches. Now sure, this didn't bother you when you were on ground level, but that wasn't always the case. We often found ourselves going around a corner with a 1,000-foot drop-off into a canyon—and it was usually on my side. If one rock moved, we were history.

Our group was laughing and screaming—that was the way we covered up our fear. It was the same kind of noise that you would hear at a roller coaster—except we were not on a track.

Despite this, the scenery was breathtaking and worth the trip until . . . we stopped. The truck shifted gears, then we stopped again. The next thing I knew, our tour guide told us all to get out of the vehicle. We did so readily. Our truck had found itself in an awkward spot. We had been driving around the side of a hill on one of those tight paths. On the left was a twenty-foot drop off. On the right was the eroded wall that made for the base of the hill. The problem was, part of the path had fallen into the river. There was no way that truck was going across, and there was no way it could be backed out. We were stuck in the Judean Wilderness!

The bus driver quickly got out and began to dig out some of the mountainside hoping to widen the path. He dug and dug and dug; however he quit too soon. He thought he had carved enough space to get by. We all told him he hadn't, but he was determined and wouldn't listen to us ignorant American tourists. He got back in the truck as our group watched from the hillside. He revved the engine and got one wheel across. We all gasped in disbelief. We were all showing our optimistic spirit by saying, "He's not going to make it." Well, we were right. He gunned the motor and the back tire fell off the path, pulling the entire truck over the side. A spare tire under the truck caught on the corner of the path and kept the vehicle from falling into the river. The back left tire was hanging over the edge of the cliff, and the front right tire was four feet off the ground. This vehicle, needless to say, was out of commission. Here we were, thirty of us, stranded in the desert heat without any civilization for miles.

Our bus driver decided to turn to the resources that Moses would have used—a cellular telephone. He phoned his boss for another truck. The unfortunate news: It would be three hours. So we did the only thing we could do. We waited and thanked God we weren't in that truck. Little did we know the incredible things God would teach us in the wilderness.

We encountered the heat and the lack of vegetation, better under-

standing why the Israelites grumbled. We experienced the hilly panorama, fully comprehending how easy it would be to get lost, even for forty years. Then God gave us a special treat. Over one hill a shepherd boy made his way down the hill, and with him came his large flock of sheep and goats. They grazed before us for the remainder of our stay. I watched closely, as God taught me how a shepherd trains his sheep.

The shepherd carried only one thing, his stick—or more biblically called his rod. The desert supplied the only other tool he would use—rocks. The area where the sheep were grazing was very hazardous. There were many cliffs and the ground was rocky and unstable. If the sheep were left to themselves, they would be in great danger. Hence, the shepherd boy stayed near. He was their protector and it was essential that they see him as their authority and guide.

As sheep would test their independence and begin to wander from the flock, the shepherd would do a most interesting thing. He would pick up a sizable rock and throw it from a great distance in front of the sheep. It would startle the sheep and it would usually jump and turn back around.

Sometimes the sheep persisted closer to a cliff in search of food. The shepherd would again pick up a rock, this time casting it closer to the sheep. Half of the time the rock would bounce and hit the sheep in a number of places. The other half of the time it would bounce away from the sheep and roll down the hill. In either case the sheep would usually turn around. When the rock would hit the sheep, it would cry out in pain. This was painful punishment, but vital for their well-being.

Occasionally, there would arise the strong-willed sheep. In this case, the shepherd would do one of two things. First, he would pick up a rock and throw it directly at the sheep, striking it on the back. If the shepherd was close enough, he would usually resort to his second option. This was to take his rod and strike the sheep several times until he turned in the other direction. In either case, the sheep got the painful message that the shepherd was in charge.

This story is a beautiful illustration of my point. The rocks and the rod represented authority and power. Other options were tried first, but when they failed to get the message across, the shepherd resorted to painful punishment.

> *The rocks and the rod represented authority and power.*

Pain had a rather swift way of redirecting their will. That little piece of grass next to the cliff suddenly lost its luster. Rebellious independence had been transformed into utter dependence. I was beginning to see what God meant when he said in Proverbs 22:15, "Folly is bound up in the heart of a child, but the rod of discipline will drive it far from him" (NIV).

After all, this was the method God said He would use in order to correct men from their evil ways. In 2 Samuel 7:14, God pledges His covenant with David: "I will be his Father, and he shall be My son. If he commits iniquity, I will chasten him with the rod of men." God clearly approves of painful punishment. But why? Because it works.

Notice this verse in 1 Corinthians 11:32, "But when we are judged, we are chastened by the Lord, that we may not be condemned with the world." God had rather give us some limited pain now in order to get us headed in the right direction than to let us continue in our path that will ultimately be total destruction. Some pain now is better than a lot of pain later.

> *God has given you the authority to use painful punishment with your child because it works.*

Sure it is going to hurt. Sure it is going to be painful for both you and your child. The Bible says in Hebrews 12:11, "Now no chastening seems to be joyful for the present, but painful; nevertheless, afterward it yields the peaceable fruit of righteousness to those who have been trained by it."

God has given you the authority to use painful punishment with your child because it works. The rod is the instrument of correction used by the shepherd over his sheep; it is also a technique of parenting that needs to be introduced to many parents with uncontrollable children.

The Myths About Painful Punishment

A great debate rages in America today, much of which is taking place in the courtroom, over the issue of spanking. Most liberals and many conservatives are fighting to take away your right to spank your child. I have a pamphlet published by The Positive Line and written by David Rubin, Ph.D. entitled *The Basics of Effective Discipline.*[1] One section of this pamphlet is named "Six Dangers of Using Physical Punishment on Children." I want to address each of these and in doing so I hope to expose the myths that this movement is built upon.

Myth #1: "You teach your children that they can control others by using intimidation and physical force."

Folks, I've got news for you: You *can* control others by using intimidation and physical force. To teach them otherwise would be denying a fact of life. I agree—it is not the best choice, but sometimes it is the only choice. To teach your children that it is not an option is robbing authorities of their authority.

Let me put this another way. The presidency of the United States is a position of authority. It is a position of authority because that position retains an enormous amount of power. If you take away the power of the President, he would cease to have authority. In addition, Americans would lose their respect for the position of President because they would no longer revere the power of that authority. By removing spanking as an option for parents, you have stripped them of much of their power. Consequently, the respect and honor due to parents vanish.

Can you imagine taking guns away from police officers? After all, a child might see the gun and think that you can control others by using intimidation and physical force. On the contrary, the gun in the hands of an officer is a great prevention of crime. The simple fact that the police officer has a gun in his arsenal eliminates much of the crime that would be possible if it were taken away. People respect that weapon. Children will respect the rod of correction.

Myth #2: "You discourage your children from resolving conflicts by reasoning and negotiating."

We must not spare the rod, but we must be very careful how and when we use it. It should be the option of last resort. Try negotiating, try rewards, try as many techniques as you can. But sometimes, you resort to painful action to get their attention. That is how the world works.

The people who are trying to resolve conflicts only by reasoning and negotiating are going to lose the big battles. They need to study some world history: People fight for their beliefs. There never has been a period of time in the history of the world where war has not been an option. These people are foolish to think they are going to change the nature of human beings and bring peace to the world by not spanking their children. Instead, they will train their children that through mere words all the problems of the world can be solved. This is ludicrous.

A servant will not be corrected by mere words; for though he understands, he will not respond.

Proverbs 29:19 explicitly says, "A servant will not be corrected by mere words; for though he understands, he will not respond." What that is saying is this: There are times when you can use all the rationale you have with your children, yet it will do no good. Your child will understand completely that the decision he will make is wrong in the eyes of his parents, yet he will do it anyway because there is no fear of punishment. Mere words are not enough. Don't let anyone tell you otherwise.

Myth #3: "You increase the chance that your children may be abusive to their own children."

The world does not know the difference between spanking and child abuse. Corporal punishment in the hands of loving parents does not lead to brutality or aggressive behavior any more than normal healthy relations between a husband and a wife lead to perverted sex and pornography.

Myth #3 would be true if we were talking about child abuse. Children who are abused are more likely to be abusive. However, the comparison they have made is a classic case of twisting the facts. SPANKING IS NOT CHILD ABUSE!!!

Corporal punishment in the hands of loving parents does not lead to brutality or aggressive behavior any more than normal healthy relations between a husband and a wife lead to perverted sex and pornography.

Now I realize a lot of people want to eliminate spanking in order to stop child abuse. That is throwing the baby out with the bath water. Child abuse is horrible, and perpetrators need to be severely punished in a prison setting for doing so. However, do not eliminate physical discipline that is done in the best interest of the child. Don't obliterate something so positive as discipline in hopes of eliminating something so horrific as abuse. There is no difference in doing this than there is in banning sex to eliminate pornography. It just doesn't make any sense.

Myth #4: "You make it more likely that your children will become rebellious toward you when they reach adolescence."

The Bible says just the opposite. Proverbs 22:15 says, "Folly is bound up in the heart of a child, but the rod of discipline will drive it far from him" (NIV). Now do you want to believe what God says will work, or do you want to believe the agenda of some people trying to promote permissiveness?

Supporters use corporal punishment because it works. For instance, one can look at the crime records of many of the Arabian countries. If you steal in Saudi Arabia, they will cut off your hands at the wrist without even a trial. As a result of this, Saudi Arabia has one of the lowest crime rates in the world. Citizens can leave their expensive belongings lying on the sidewalk without any fear of loss. Why? Because corporal punishment works.

Discipline with love will not promote rebellion. Discipline without love may. But if you choose not to correct your child, rebellion and self-destruction are almost always certain. Someone has well said, "A good father, finding his son on the wrong track, will provide switching facilities."[2]

Myth #5: "You make it less likely that your children will develop a sensitivity to the feelings of others."

There is absolutely no evidence or basis for this quote. Don't let them play some psychological mind game with you. Spanking your child for breaking the rules has nothing to do with the sensitivity to the feelings of others. This is simply a ploy for them to attack you at an emotional level. "If you spank your kids, they will grow up to be tough and mean," declares the liberal. I ask you to consider one thought: "Do you believe that gang members were properly disciplined and spanked before they became gang members?" Of course not. Yet, they consistently commit some of the most gruesome crimes imaginable, and their victims are often innocent people. By not doing everything possible, including spanking, to drive your child to an honorable path, you are setting him up to destroy himself and other innocent people who are standing along the way.

Myth #6: "You can seriously harm your children and possibly face criminal charges."

Again, I want to say, we must not spare the rod, but we must be very careful how and when we use it. Discipline should never be done in the midst of parental anger. Make sure you are in control of yourself before you try to get control of your child. Think before you act. God is very clear as to the proper place where the instrument of discipline should be applied. Proverbs 10:13 says, "A rod is for the back of him who is devoid of understanding." Now, there is no provision in the Bible giving you the right to slap your child on the face. However, there is provision for you applying needed discipline to his or her buttocks. When spanking is needed as a last resort, the proper place is on the seat of the pants.

Now, I cannot predict how the future court system will rule on these matters of spanking. If we go on its past history, the day may come when spanking is outlawed. I spoke as an authority on this issue on a radio talk show from Dayton, Ohio, concerning an actual court case. A father had been taken to court by his wife because he paddled his ten-year-old boy. After it was clear that the father had not abused the child, the judge wanted to make an issue out of the situation. This good father was found guilty of paddling his child and for his punishment, the judge had the thirty-three-year-old father paddled in front of everyone. That judge made a mockery of the court system. This is just an example of how far down our courts have gone.

It was quite interesting what occurred on the talk show. I spoke as the authority to defend spanking, but they could not find anyone else who was confident enough to defend the other side. This just shows that the majority of people believe in spanking. But if we are not careful, this minority who doesn't is going to rule the multitudes.

Reward vs. Punishment

Do more people talk about the blessings of God, or the punishments of God? No matter what your age is, we all learn better through rewards than punishments. As Martin Luther expressed it, "Next to the rod must lie the apple."[3]

During a time of famine in France, a rich man invited twenty of the poor children in the town to his house, and said to them, "In this basket is a loaf for each one of you; take it, and come back every day at this hour till God sends us better times." The children pounced upon the basket, wrangled, and fought for the bread. Each wished to get the largest loaf, and at last went away without thanking their friend. Francesca alone, a poor but neatly dressed girl, stood modestly apart, took the smallest loaf which was left in the basket, gracefully kissed the gentleman's hand, and went away to her home in a quiet and becoming manner. On the following day the children were equally ill-behaved, and Francesca this time received a loaf that was scarcely half the size of the others. But when she got home her sick mother cut the loaf, and there fell out of it a number of bright silver coins. The mother was alarmed, and said, "Take back the money this instant, for it has no doubt got into the bread by some mistake." Francesca carried it back, but the benevolent gentleman declined to receive it. "No, no," said he, "it was no mistake. I had the money baked in the smallest loaf simply as a reward for you, my good child. Always continue thus contented, peaceable, and unassuming. The person who prefers to remain content with the smallest loaf, rather than quarrel for the larger one, will find throughout life blessings in this course of action still more valuable than the money which was baked in your loaf of bread."[4]

Instead of taking good behavior for granted, be enthusiastic when your child does as you ask. Good behavior that receives no attention is less likely to be repeated. Reinforce positive behavior with a reward. You may consider ignoring bad behavior occasionally in order to achieve the desired response. Look away and stop verbal communication until your request is granted, then immediately affirm and praise his actions. While you are ignoring the child, he may cry, and that is permissible. He will learn soon enough that obedience makes the atmosphere good.

Be careful that the rewards are good for them. Candy, cokes, and cookie dough are probably not the best payback for proper behavior.

> *Candy, cokes, and cookie dough are probably not the best payback for proper behavior.*

While rewards are a very good teaching method, they will not replace the need for punishment. Punishment, especially spanking, is used after the reward method has lost its effectiveness. You may want to hang up a reminder to your child that punishment is always an option for misbehavior. I would suggest rolling up a newspaper and placing it on top of the refrigerator. Let it stick out just a bit so that it can serve as a constant reminder to your child to pursue excellent conduct.

You may want to hang up both rewards and punishments. After all, that is what God usually does. He says if you do this, I will bless you; if you do that, I will punish you. Let your child have that option as well.

Vary Your Method of Discipline

It is important not to let the discipline of your children become a routine—a habit—a reaction. Don't find one thing that works and use just that. You want to keep your child guessing.

You certainly don't want to spank your child for every incident of misbehavior. Spanking will lose its effectiveness if it is used constantly. Your child will have good days and bad days, just like you. You will need something severe to get his attention on the bad days. That is where spanking will pay off. However, if you pop him on the leg for every little action, you will not have this method to use. Its repetition will wear off its effectiveness. Then, you will find yourself confused, frustrated, and befuddled.

Therefore, use variety. There are some general techniques that may be used in several different situations. In the next chapter, we will discuss particular problems and how they can be handled. But for now, here are some generalities.

Distracting

This method simply tries to divert the child's attention in another direction. For instance, you may be at church and the child is making noise. At this point, pull out a toy from your purse and hopefully his attention will turn to this newfound enjoyment.

Negotiating

This type of discipline is basically saying, "If you won't do that, I'll let you do this." Some people might call this a bribe, but it is not. Charles "Tremendous" Jones explains well the difference between a bribe and a reward. "A bribe is giving someone something to do evil. A reward is giving someone something to do good." He follows this with a story about a father and his son. When the child reached the age where he could readily read, the father offered him a prop-

> *"A bribe is giving someone something to do evil. A reward is giving someone something to do good."*

osition. He said, "Son, when you are sixteen you are going to want a car. I want you to be able to have a car. I will put $10 in a separate car account for every book that you read. When you reach sixteen, you will receive that account for a car. Son, if you read like a bum, you will drive like a bum. But if you read like a winner, you will drive like a winner."⁵ Now this was a good healthy reward for the son. This is negotiating used effectively.

Ignoring

While this technique should be used sparingly, nonetheless, it can be used. This process involves the parents' turning their heads and looking in the other direction, overlooking the deed. Oftentimes the child misbehaves in order to get your attention. This technique is effective in demonstrating to your child that proper behavior will get your attention much better than improper behavior.

Communicating

Another important generality concerning discipline is to communicate with your child after the punishment. The time varies depending upon the extent of the punishment, the severity of the deed, or the sensitivity of the child. You must gain the child's affection after the emotion of the situation is over. This is discipline with love. After I had spanked my children, I would usually hold them until they quit crying, regardless of how long it took. They would struggle and I would just hold them. When they finally quit struggling and quieted down, I would explain that I had to do this because I loved them. This would usually lead to a very sweet time of understanding and love—a bonding time for parent and child.

There are many other methods you may want to try. Be creative. Overall, **keep punishments at a minimum.** For the most part, make them **short, meaningful, different,** and they should be **related in time** as closely as possible to the wrongdoing. But, of course, just like any other rule, there are exceptions. This will serve as a good guide for you.

Speaking of short punishment, one day a mother came into the office bragging about the punishment she had given to her two-year-old son. "No TV for one month!" Now a two-year-old cannot comprehend discipline for that length of time. I think she should have selected a more reasonable or appropriate punishment for that age child.

Especially for younger children, keep the punishment short and close to the time of offense. As they grow older, you may use more variety. I vividly recall an encounter with my older son at the barber shop. Following his haircut, I instructed him to sit still in the chair and not run around while I was getting my hair cut. But as children will do, no sooner had I settled back in the barber's chair, when my son jumped up, moving from chair to chair, running to the coke machine and then to the peanut machine. I reprimanded him several times, but he never acknowledged hearing me.

As I was paying for the haircuts, he came and stood close to my side. (Sound familiar?) Very calmly, I told him that I wanted him to go to the bathroom when he got home. My son immediately replied, "Dad, I don't have to go to the bathroom." He had always sat in the front seat with me, but on that particular day, he rode standing on the back floor leaning over the front seat. Several times on the way home he would say, "Really, Dad, I don't have to go to the bathroom."

As I was getting out of the car, he said, "Dad, I'm not going to get out of the car right now." I assured him, "That's okay, but when you do get out, go straight to the bathroom." As I entered the back door, my wife asked me where he was. I responded, "Well, he's in the car but soon he will be coming in, and when he does, he will be going straight to the bathroom." And sure enough, it wasn't long until he came in and headed straight for the bathroom. I followed and applied some much-needed discipline.

Usually I dealt with the punishment immediately, but on that occasion, I decided to postpone it. It afforded my son an opportunity to think of what he had done. However, the problem with postponing punishment is, it is too easy to forget or let the punishment slide by. I would not use this option when children are very young.

If it is possible, let your child's punishment reflect the situation. Let me give you an example that occurred with our daughter, who was in preschool at the time. My wife had taken her to the grocery. When they returned to the car, my wife noticed my little girl shyly opening a piece of candy. She had stolen it from the grocery store. Now a number of discipline techniques could be applied here, but my wife was wise in choosing one that would not only reflect the situation, but it would be a punishment our daughter would remember to this day. She went back into the store and asked to see the manager. Our daughter's punishment was to return it and apologize. This provided enough humiliation and tears to make her think several times before she would again take something that didn't belong to her.

So remember, keep the punishments at a minimum; keep them short, meaningful, and different; and keep them as close to the time of wrongdoing as possible.

A word about spanking

With a great variety of effective punishment techniques, you may wonder when to spank. I would recommend the following rule of thumb to be applied. Before painful punishment is used, several positive punishments should be attempted. Some of those options may include rewards, time-out, not visiting the grandparents, or not going outside. When these do not work, painful punishment will usually get their attention. There is one exception to this. If a child openly defies your authority, spanking should be a first choice. Some children will do this only a couple of times in their lives; others will every week. But you can count on every child's doing it at some point. Painful punishment is appropriate and expected.

Let me give you an example of defying your authority. Suppose a father and son were wrestling and running around the house and the child accidentally knocked over a lamp. In this case, I would not punish the child. However, if the father asked the child to pick up his shoes and take them to his room, and the child instead reached down and threw his shoes at the lamp, breaking it, that would be a different story. Now in either case, the lamp is broken. Yet in the second incident, the child is clearly defying the father's authority and is worthy of some love licks on his backside. Parents, I encourage you to look at the intent of the heart. There you will find the justification you are looking for to punish your children properly.

I encourage you to look at the intent of the heart.

Forms of discipline never to use

There are other forms of discipline that may be detrimental to the child. They may leave permanent and lasting scars. Three of these in particular are **sarcasm**, **ridicule**, and **nagging**. We should abstain from using these forms of discipline at any time under any circumstance. They have no place in the proper training of children.

Age-Specific Discipline

A common frustration that I often hear from a mother is knowing the appropriate expectations of her child's age. She is confused as to what level of conduct the child is capable of maintaining. This leads to further puzzlement in determining when and how to discipline.

My good friend, Dr. James Dobson, has provided us with an age-level guideline for expectations and punishments.[6] I want to expand on these basic divisions.

Birth to 7 months

If you start training your child the day after he is born, you are one day too late. I like to refer to these first seven months as training more than discipline. Discipline often carries with it a tone of punishment. You are NOT to punish your child during these months, simply because he will not understand what that means. The chief objective at this age is to establish who is in control. This is,

> *If you start training your child the day after he is born, you are one day too late.*

first of all, implemented by feeding and sleeping patterns. These begin at day one. I will discuss this more fully in the next chapter. You don't want the baby to control you. Instead, you want to be in control of the baby. Remember the mother of the two-week-old who called and said that he would not let her take his temperature. He was two weeks old. Who would you say is in control? This is what we want to avoid.

Your child's training is sufficient in these months if he learns that you are there to meet his needs, that you love him, but that you are in control, and that he can't have everything he wants when he wants it.

8 to 14 months

During these months your child will develop to the stage that he can fully understand the word "NO!" One of the hardest jobs for a parent is making a child realize that "NO" is a complete sentence. He will probably hear it more in these seven months than he will all the rest of his life. But that's okay. When your child gets involved in something that he shouldn't, you should tell him, "No." Be persistent. If after several warnings, he doesn't quit, the appropriate response is to physically pick him up and carry him to another place. This reaffirms who is in control. Physically carrying a child is a good discipline technique that can be used until they are six or seven. Penelope Leach says,

> *Physically carrying a small child reinforces—in a positive way— what you've said, provided you do it before a complaint has turned into an argument or an argument into a tantrum. If you have a six- or seven-year-old who finds it embarrassing to be carried, he'll understand that he can easily avoid it by doing what you ask under his own power.*[7]

15 to 24 months

This is usually the time when children will begin to fight for their rights. The battles will begin. Your task is to win the battles early. The more battles you win at this age, the fewer battles you will have to win when they grow older. At this age, a good technique to use for discipline is time-out. Don't make it too long, maybe ten minutes. Remember your child is small and cannot comprehend a long duration of time. It is essential that you win those very first encounters when the child challenges your authority as a parent. If you don't, you are going to have trouble in the future.

It is essential that you win those very first encounters when the child challenges your authority as a parent.

I recall a classic case—a ten-year-old boy named Fred. In all honesty, the staff and I dreaded to see Fred enter the door. He was an undisciplined, destructive, defiant creature, looking for accidents to happen. One day during a physical examination on Fred, I discovered severe cavities in his teeth. I knew he must be referred to a dentist, but to whom? With fear of ending a professional friendship, I selected an elderly dentist who had experienced many difficulties with unruly children through the years.

The conflict started the day Fred and his mother arrived at the dentist's office. She remained in the waiting room reading her *Better Homes and Gardens* magazine while Fred and the dentist were in the treatment room. "Get in the chair, son," said the dentist. "No," was Fred's defiant answer. "I said get in the chair, now." Fred replied, "I will take off all my clothes, if you make me get in that chair." "Take them off, then—I'm waiting," the doctor said. Reluctantly, the boy removed his shirt, undershirt, socks, and shoes. Then the dentist insisted that he get in the chair. But angrily Fred said, "I will take off all my clothes." "Then take them off son." Fred continued his striptease act, removing his pants and then his shorts. He stood there stark naked to the amazement of the dentist and his assistant. "Now, get in the chair," said the dentist. Fred climbed into the chair and patiently endured the entire procedure. As he stepped down from the chair, Fred said, "Now, give me my clothes."

"No, I'm sorry," replied the dentist. "Your mother may pick them up tomorrow." As the door opened into the waiting room and Fred's mother saw her ten-year-old son standing in his birthday suit before a room filled with patients, can you imagine her shock?

Mother and naked son walked into the hall, down a public elevator and into a large parking lot to find their car. Fred had lost his battle!

The following day Fred's mother returned to the dentist's office and requested to speak with him. She was so grateful for what the dentist had done to help her with her problem. Then she shared the following story with him:

"For years Fred has been threatening to remove his clothes in public places if I didn't comply with his wants and wishes. It might be in a grocery store and he had asked for candy. If I refused, he would say, 'If you don't buy it, I'll take off all my clothes.'" Over and over Fred had used this to manipulate his mother.

The impact that this incident made in Fred's life was incredible. It is imperative that children have parental leadership. Win those battles early, so that you will not have to deal with this when they are older. The battles are much easier to win when they are young.

24 to 48 months

This is the period more commonly known as the "terrible twos," "threatening threes," and "ferocious fours." Before the child is four years of age, Dr. Dobson says, there are two vital messages that need to be delivered to your child. The first, "I love you more than you can possibly understand." The child needs to understand that he is loved unconditionally by his parents. Second, "Because I love you, I must teach you to obey me."[8] Communicate to your child that your laws are for their benefit, and they arise out of your undying love for them. If you can impart these to them while they are young, you will be well on your way to training a winning child.

4 to 8 years old

During these years, you will learn a lot about your child. You will begin to detect his love language and can respond accordingly. The discipline techniques you incorporate will prove to be working or failing. You will have a lot of time to practice during these years. If a child is strong-willed, his determination will blossom during this time. If you have won the early battles, you will reap the benefits during these years. If you have not, you will be challenged to do it the hard way. You must reassert your authority and take charge. This is your last chance before he begins to assert his independence on a large scale.

Dr. Barnhouse tells the following story:

> *An item in the* New York Times *reported a court case of a mother who brought a nine-year-old son into Juvenile Court; the boy screamed, stamped on the floor and pounded with his fists. The court psychiatrist said, "It is sheer blackmail. He screams to blackmail his mother. When he gets his own way, he stops screaming. He has been heard to tell his younger brother to*

scream for what he wants. Now the younger boy has become a kind of deputy screamer." The boy was perfectly normal at school and only screamed for his mother. The psychiatrist said, "This is an extreme case of individualism, and the symptoms are a pathological manifestation."

These are long words for what the Bible would call an outburst of the "old Adam." If the child had been spanked when he was younger and refused his own way, he would not have grown up to blackmail his mother. If the first time the child had ever screamed, he had had a sound application of the "board of education to the seat of knowledge," the screaming would not have been repeated.[9]

9 to 12 years old

At this age you should begin to recognize their independence. Your methods of discipline will usually turn from physical punishment to removal of privileges. Dr. Dobson gives an exception: "Some strong-willed children absolutely demand to be spanked, and their wishes should be granted."[10]

> *"Some strong-willed children absolutely demand to be spanked, and their wishes should be granted.*

This is a very sensitive age for a child. There is much adjustment for both the parent and the child. Do all that you can to nurture a trust relationship between you and your child. Tell him often that you are giving him this new opportunity, this new freedom, this privilege, because you trust him. If you can get him to value your trust, far fewer problems will develop in the teen-age years.

In summary, discipline isn't a hard-and-fast set of rules that will work with all children. What I have given you are principles—principles that work. Don't stop at the point of learning what generally works. Go beyond that and get to know your child, and see what works with him. Children vary in their response to discipline. Some are sensitive, some are tough-minded. Discipline is for the parents as well as for the children. Remember, it is the authoritative tool God has given you to train them. Use it wisely, use it cautiously, but use it. Your children are counting on it.

Common Mistakes in Discipline

Inconsistency

Someone has well said, "Youngsters don't rebel at discipline; they do rebel at inconsistency."[11] This is one of the foundational rules of discipline. Don't say one thing and then do another. Model before them a consistent standard. One person said, "No matter how much I rant and rave, I just can't get my children to behave rationally."

It was a "no-no" in the family for the child to touch the knobs on the television. Each time the child did this he was scolded, punished, and reprimanded. One day the minister came for a visit. As the mother and minister were chatting, suddenly Junior burst into the room. He sized up the situation very quickly and knew he was not to touch the knobs. He marched straight to the television and began turning each and every knob. The mother looked at the minister and said, "What a smart boy he is. He knows all the knobs on the television." No reprimand, no scolding, no punishment: This is inconsistent discipline.

Don't let the guilty go unpunished. Prepare yourself for these circumstances. Children are brilliant in knowing how to assess the situation. Be prepared in advance, and catch them in the act.

Idle threats

How well I remember Mrs. Martin and her three boys, Jimmy, Kyle, and Derek. To say they were undisciplined is a masterpiece of an understatement. They were out of control. These children were so disruptive they had been banned from the local shopping mall where her husband worked. It was such a joy to see them come into the office. (I hope you can detect my sarcasm.) They would tear up everything on which they could get their hands. My office staff would gather at the check-in window and watch in amazement as Mrs. Martin would try to control her boys. The frequent scene they would observe from behind the nurse's station was Mrs. Martin standing in front of the three seated boys with a yard stick in her hand, whopping them every time they moved.

One child during every examination had a rather puzzling performance. When the announcement was made to the child that the nurse would be right in (meaning that he was going to receive a shot), little Jimmy, age six, would take off running. He would run out of the building, down the street, past the grocery store, around a fast food restaurant and continue right back to the office, to the treatment room, and would willfully hop back up on the table to then receive his shot. It was truly amazing. No one ran after him, because we all knew he would be back.

The children received warnings, but no corrections. The result was—no training.

Anyway, I tell you this story to now share with you what was missing in Mrs. Martin's discipline. She threatened her boys. Over and over she would tell them what she was going to do if they didn't behave. The problem was, she would never follow through. The children received warnings, but no corrections. The result was—no training.

One parent does all of the discipline

I want to introduce you to Ashley. There are few patients that so easily embrace one's heart. The first time that I met Ashley was a grievous occasion. Her mother brought her in to the office at two months of age with the belief that her child had a little cold. Ashley was the last patient of the day, and as I walked into treatment room number three, I froze. There was Ashley, white as snow. My immediate reaction was to think the worst, but I hoped so very, very much that it wouldn't be true. Of course, I did not present my alarm to Ashley's mother until we had done some extensive tests. That night, however, we were regrettably able to confirm—Ashley had leukemia.

The next five years, we would see Ashley a lot. We watched her grow up. We admired her as she fought courageously a battle that was unjustly and unsparingly cruel to her small frame. Every week she would come in for her injections. She was a beautiful child with a warm, outgoing personality. I fell in love with Ashley and she did so with me. We had a bond; I was on her team.

But this was not the case between Miss Ann, my head nurse, and the adorable little Ashley. Ashley hated Miss Ann, in the truest sense of the word. I want to tell you of Ashley's story, not to make any negative references to her parents—they were loving and strong supports for Ashley during her illness. But I want to draw a parallel between Ashley's story and the principles that emerge when one parent does all of the discipline. However, I am going to substitute Ann and myself for Ashley's parents. What made the difference between Ashley's loving me and hating Miss Ann? I will tell you that Ann is one of the sweetest, most compassionate women God ever made. So the hinge of Ashley's door of love did not swing on personality. What made the difference?

Well, let's get on with Ashley's story. When she would come into the office, she would usually run down the halls to the back room, climb under the conference table, and pull the chairs in behind her. She hated those injections, they hurt, and it grieved us to see her in pain. But sooner or later, Ashley would come out and Miss Ann would give her the medicine. After she was done, Ashley would come charging back to my office, jump in my lap, and give me a big hug. She would cry, and I would hold her tightly. Ann would stick her head in my office to see if everything was okay. Ashley would say emphatically with her lisp, "I hate choo Mith Ann!!" Then she would look at me and say, "Mith Ann's not on our team." I would explain that Miss Ann was just trying to get her well and that she was very much a part of the team. But this was so hard for Ashley to see, because the sight of Miss Ann always meant pain in her little mind.

I am happy to report that after five long years of battling the disease, Ashley won. She is doing fine now and is actively pursuing her life. But I want to ask the question again: "Why did she love me, and hate Miss Ann?" I hope it is easy for you to see by now. I represented comfort and love; Miss Ann was discomfort and pain.

Many parents make the mistake of choosing one person to do all of the discipline and punishment. Your child may develop the tendency of seeing one of you as the disciplinarian and the other as a refuge. This can cause a great deal of problems in maintaining unity between the parents.

Let me give you some helpful advice concerning this. Statistics tell us that seventy percent of all discipline is done by the mother. This stands to reason because mothers are at home with children more often. I do not encourage mothers to wait until their husbands get home for discipline to be enforced. Discipline should almost always be immediately following the crime. Don't ever say, "Your Dad will take care of you when he gets home." It's not fair to the child, and it is certainly not fair to Dad. But when Dad is at home, I usually recommend that he administer the discipline. This allows the child to see a balance between Mom and Dad. Both are capable of punishing. Neither is a refuge when the child is in need of discipline.

Tyrant mentality

God's Word says in Colossians 3:21, "Fathers, do not provoke your children, lest they become discouraged." If there is too much authority and punishment in the child's life, he will become negative and rebellious. We see this often in working parents who come home tired and worn out. The last thing they need is to have to deal with the squabbles and complaints that accompany children. They get angry and the punishments are handed out like tickets at the fair.

Most children can handle discipline that says they were wrong about something specific, but it is so hard for them to handle discipline that diminishes their feelings of self-worth. They can accept a strong, firm rebuke about something that was clearly a family rule or standard. But punishment given unfairly—if they have no chance to explain, or if they had not known in advance that what they did was wrong—creates discouragement. This makes it hard for them to receive that punishment—and rightly so.

Parents often use anger to get action, especially when they are tired. I encourage you to use action to get action. The principles of the past three chapters have sought to show you how. Use them.

The Apostle Paul warns parents again in Ephesians 6:4, "And you, fathers, do not provoke your children to wrath, but bring them up in the training and admonition of the Lord."

Chapter 8

What Do I Do
When . . . ?
(Infancy)

*My son, do not despise the chastening of the LORD,
Nor be discouraged when you are rebuked by Him;
For whom the LORD loves He chastens,
And scourges every son whom He receives.*

HEBREWS 12:5-6

Folks, it's time to get what I want to call "intensely practical." First, we want to begin by learning how to care for that newborn and infant. "What is the best way to get my child to sleep all night?" "What should I feed him?" "When should I feed him?" "Should I breast feed or bottle feed, use scheduled or demand feedings?" "What are the basics in caring for my new little baby?" Answers to these questions and many more are what this chapter is all about. These solutions are tried and proven, and I promise you they work.

What to Ask on the Prenatal Visit

You will soon find out, if you haven't already, that after having a child, your pediatrician will be like a member of your family. He or she will be the walking answer to most of your frustration and fear when it comes to the health and welfare of your baby. Therefore, it is very important that you choose a pediatrician who will naturally agree with your philosophy and wishes. I have compiled a list of questions that you may want to cover with your candidate pediatrician on your prenatal visit that hopefully will help you in making your decision. This prenatal visit should be made approximately two months before your baby is due.

1. How quickly do you return phone calls? Do you or does your nurse return the calls?
2. Do you prefer a mother to bottle or breast feed?
3. What is your feeding schedule for babies?
4. When do you start solid foods for babies?
5. What is your philosophy on the proper discipline of children?
6. Do you believe in painful punishment when given in love?
7. What are your office hours?
8. Do you have a certain time in the day to see "sick children" and a certain time to see "well children"?
9. Do you give antibiotics over the phone?
10. Does your clinic do lab procedures, make x-rays, give allergy shots, or suture lacerations?
11. What hospitals do you use?

12. Where do I go in case of an emergency at night, holidays, or weekends?

13. Do you accept my insurance?

14. Ask for a tour of the office. Things to notice: Is it clean and orderly? Do the personnel seem happy and friendly toward you? Is it overall a very professional atmosphere?

After leaving the office, ask your friends and neighbors what their opinions are of that pediatrician and his office. It is important to feel comfortable with the other pediatricians in the office as well, because sooner or later, they will be on call when your child has an emergency.

Before Coming Home from the Hospital

Breast vs. Bottle Feeding

Bottom line, the mother alone should make the decision as to whether to breast feed or bottle feed her newborn. This is not a decision for the in-laws, the mother's mother, or even the pediatrician. A good pediatrician will abide by the wishes of the mother and help her to accomplish the feeding of her choice. I have noticed that in my four decades of practice the pendulum preference keeps swinging. When I first started, most mothers bottle fed. Later on the pendulum swung to favor breast feeding. At my most recent observation, about fifty percent of my patients were bottle feeding and fifty percent were breast feeding. If it is possible, it would be my recommendation to start with breast feeding at least for the first three weeks. During these weeks, the majority of the antibodies will be delivered from the mom to her baby.

Breast Feeding

If you choose to breast feed, you may decide to use one breast at one feeding and alternate for the next. One drawback to this schedule of feeding is that the breast that is not used at this particular feeding will become engorged and may become painful to you. However, a plus for this method is that there will be more milk for the next feeding since the emptying of the breast will increase the production of more milk.

You may choose to use both breasts at each feeding. You start with one breast for ten minutes and alternate to the other for another ten minutes. You may not have as much milk with this routine, but the comfort level is much better. Both schedules are good and will work well for your baby. I would encourage you to try both, and then use the one that is more convenient for you and your child.

Bottle Feeding

If you choose to bottle feed, the immediate question that comes to mind is which formula. You'll find a large assortment of prepared formulas in today's market. Now, I will not endorse any of these products for profit, but I will make a recommendation strictly on the performance of the product. I prefer my patients use "Similac with low iron." I have found that most babies tolerate this product best with the least number of complications and allergies. Of course, with any of these milks, including breast milk, a baby may be allergic and an alternate milk should be used. Another reason I prefer "Similac with low iron" is because of the very fact that it uses the daily requirement of iron and no more. Brands that use a higher dosage of iron oftentimes will produce staining of permanent teeth in the infant as well as diarrhea.

Breast and Bottle Combination

Some mothers, usually those who return to work, want to breast feed but use the bottle as a supplement. Mothers can start this at any time, and I have no objection to this. The one stipulation that I would enforce is that at an individual feeding use one or the other, not both. Using both at a time has the potential to confuse the baby. In an adult's mind it is like starting a meal in the dining room, moving to the kitchen, and ending up on the patio. Babies seem not to have a problem when one complete feeding is on the bottle, and the next complete feeding is with the breast.

Circumcision

You will be faced with another decision before leaving the hospital if you have a little boy. You will be asked if you want your little baby boy to undergo circumcision. Many of you will have religious ties to this, but if not I would strongly recommend having your little boy circumcised for two reasons. First, it has been shown that there is a lower incidence of cancer in adult males who have been circumcised. The second reason is a purely practical one. Most of the other boys in the locker room will have been circumcised. Children like to pick out differences and then turn that into a joke. I have known many boys in my career who have refused to return to school because of the cruelty from the other children. This problem can easily be prevented by circumcision.

In caring for the circumcision, get a small strip of gauze with vaseline and place on the treated area. Change this wrapping during each diaper change.

Schedule vs. Demand Feedings

Demand Feedings

Simply defined, this is feeding your baby whenever **he** wants to eat. Now, from that simplistic definition, can you see demanding children as a healthy beginning in establishing authority in the home? When should you begin disciplining and training your child? My answer to that again is that if you start the second day, you are one day too late. A demand-type feeding allows your baby to control you, which encourages your baby to take small amounts of food when feeding occurs. The result of this is very simply that there is less time between feedings and more time and inconvenience placed on the mother. With demand feedings, no schedule can be set for the mom or the baby. There is absolutely no nutritional value to this system as many other pediatricians and nutritionists may espouse. Schedules make the baby happier and they certainly make Mom and Dad happier.

There is one very interesting observation I have made in my practice over the years. When I am counseling a parent over a severe discipline problem with a child, I always ask one question: "Did you feed this child on demand or by a routine?" In every case where a child is in need of a strong authority and firm discipline, the parent has always said, "Demand feeding." You, as the parent, must bring this child home from the hospital with the attitude and determination that you are going to be in authority and you are going to be in control. This is why I strongly, boldly, and emphatically recommend scheduled feedings for your baby.

Scheduled Feedings

Scheduled feedings are to be given at certain times in the day. You should begin by feeding every four hours starting at six a.m. and ending at ten p.m. **The baby should be awakened for feedings during the** daytime hours. **At night, you should not awaken the baby to feed him.** Let him awaken on his own. After the baby cries for twenty minutes, a feeding should be given. This gives the baby a chance to get good and hungry as well as an opportunity to aerate his lungs.

Scheduled feedings provide a routine for your baby. The child will adapt to this usually within the first two weeks of life. Then the baby and his parents will be much happier in the future. The most important thing is that you have set the tone for discipline and the benefits will be reaped quickly. Let's look at the following section to gain a better understanding of how all this works.

The First Two Weeks

How to get your baby to sleep all night after only two weeks

Sounds impossible, doesn't it? It's not. After forty-three years of examining newborns, one begins to see a pattern. All babies want to be in control. They want to eat on their own schedule, and they want to sleep whenever they feel like it. This is why I emphatically believe that newborns need discipline. They need to understand who is in control, and the earlier you can establish this, the better. By parental regulation of the newborn's sleeping and feeding patterns, proper training can be enforced. Let me describe to you how this has worked for thousands of my patients.

Regular sleeping and feeding patterns have a way of bringing harmony to the home. They can usually be established properly by adopting the following routine for a normal, healthy seven- to eight-pound baby. On your first day at home from the hospital, starting at six a.m., awaken your baby every four hours for the daytime feedings. Wipe his face off with cold water or thump him on the bottom of his feet in order to get him wide awake for each feeding. Your baby's stomach will then be full after the last feeding at ten p.m. Then place your child in his own room (close to mom and dad), his own bed, and turn off the light (babies are not afraid of the dark). Usually bassinets are disliked by the babies because they can't see out or breathe fresh air. Your baby should sleep on a firm mattress with bumper pads and should not be awakened during the night for feedings.

If your baby awakens at two a.m., or should I say *when* your baby awakens at two a.m., do not jump up immediately. Let your baby cry for fifteen to twenty minutes in the hope that he may drop back to sleep. If he doesn't, these fifteen minutes will give him the opportunity to get wide awake and develop a good appetite. Then proceed with another feeding. If you do not allow for such an interval, your baby will take a small amount of feeding, drop off to sleep for an hour or so, and then repeat the process. You will be getting up every hour, on the hour. Each night this process is applied, your baby will usually extend the time he sleeps by twenty or thirty minutes. By two weeks of age, most babies will be sleeping all night between ten p.m. and six a.m. At six a.m., the baby should be awakened for his first scheduled feeding.

Mothers often tell me that they don't object to getting up with their babies at night, but they soon realize they are encouraging the infants' undesirable sleeping habits. Some new mothers are fearful that they may not be able to distinguish between their children's cries of hunger and their cries of pain. This is understandable, but let me put your mind at ease. There is a distinct difference between these two cries. Mothers have a better radar system for this than the fathers. Trust my years of experience: You'll know the difference. God has designed it that way. If you have trouble in distinguishing between cries of pain and cries of want, I guarantee you will know the difference after your child has received his two-weeks' immunizations.

Approximately ninety percent of all the new mothers that I have seen in my practice who followed this schedule, rarely get up with their infants. After the first two weeks, babies slept all night, mothers slept all night, and both felt better the following morning. In my opinion, if your baby controls his schedule after two weeks of age, you have started the training process off on the wrong foot.

Feeding specifics

If you are breast feeding, I encourage you to begin with five- to six-minute feedings when you first bring your baby home from the hospital. You will increase over the next three to four days to about twenty minutes' nursing time. If your baby is bottle feeding, you will begin with two ounces and increase as the baby desires. Never let the baby suck on an empty bottle. In both cases, you should begin feeding the baby every three hours and increase to every four hours as soon as possible. The sooner you can get your baby on the four-hour feeding schedule in the daytime, the sooner you will see your baby sleeping all night. Let the baby take as much milk as he desires. Remember, all these suggestions on feeding are for normal, full-term, healthy babies. If there is variance from this, you should consult with your personal pediatrician.

Cord Care

Caring for the umbilical cord frightens many parents. I believe some basic care instructions can eliminate most of those fears. You should wipe the cord completely with each diaper change using rubbing alcohol. Don't be afraid of moving the cord around and wiping underneath the cord. Most babies cry with this procedure, but it is because the cold alcohol is being applied to the warm tummy. Don't worry if after a few days the cord is knocked off. Also don't intentionally try to pull the cord off. Sooner or later, usually after two weeks, the cord will fall off on its own. You should continue to use the alcohol for several more days. There may be some bleeding but this is perfectly normal.

Bathing

Many mothers anxiously await the day they can bathe their little baby. These suggestions may again offer some peace of mind. Until the cord has completely come off and has been off for several days, you should not put the baby in water. A sponge bath, without soap, is completely adequate until this has occurred. Following the cord removal, the baby usually will love his bath if you hold him securely in the water. Only soap may be used at this time, and I would suggest using Dial or other hypoallergenic soaps. Oils and lotions should not be used due to the fact that a large number of babies are allergic to them. The exception to this is A & D ointment, which I recommend for diaper rash.

Illnesses

Diarrhea/Constipation

It is, first of all, important to know that you do not determine diarrhea or constipation based on the number of stools a baby has in a day. A baby could have loose or very frequent stools and still be constipated or impacted.

We determine diarrhea and constipation in a baby based on the consistency of the stool. Normal stools have the consistency of putty. The color of the stools may vary, but it is usually light brown in color. Children do not have to have a stool every day. In fact, it is perfectly normal to have several putty-looking stools daily or even have a stool every five to six days.

Jaundice of the Newborn

Jaundice may not appear until two or three days after a baby is born. Therefore, since most mothers take their baby home within twenty-four hours, the baby may not appear to have this until he leaves the hospital. Jaundice is caused by the breakdown of the body's red blood cells, which contain bilirubin. The more breakdown of the red blood cells, the more bilirubin in the baby's blood. When this occurs, the baby will appear yellow in direct proportion to the level of bilirubin in the blood. Most cases can be handled with giving water (six to eight ounces daily) for a few days until the yellow color has disappeared. Another technique used is to put the baby, undressed, in direct sunlight for twenty minutes three times daily until the jaundice has disappeared. The sunlight slows down the breakdown of the red blood cells and the water helps to flush the bilirubin out of the body through the urine. If this condition occurs, you need to consult your pediatrician.

Newborn Females

In newborn females, certain conditions may appear the first few days including lumps under one or both breasts, swelling of the labia, and vaginal bleeding or discharge. All of these signs are normal and will clear up in a few days. If these conditions continue, you should consult your pediatrician.

Immunizations

It is my suggestion that your baby receive all of the immunizations approved by the American Academy of Pediatrics. These immunizations will prevent many of the childhood illnesses that in the past have caused severe health problems for children.

Grandparents and Visitors

It is natural for the grandmothers to want to come to the house to aid the new parents with their new baby. I have found that some basic rules help in this sometimes awkward situation. Lots of opinions will be floating around and this can cause frustration and confusion.

Rule #1: Mom and Dad should be the ones to decide what is best for their baby based on their discussion with their pediatrician.

Rule #2: Grandmothers on both sides need to understand that their role is to do the mopping, ironing, cooking, and cleaning of the house—NOT to care for the baby. These chores being done by the grandmothers enable the mother to care for her own baby.

Rule #3: The baby's mother needs to tell these rules to her mother before the baby comes home. This is not the father's place.

Rule #4: The baby's father needs to tell these rules to his mother before the baby comes home. This is not the mother's place.

Rule #5: When visitors come over, the baby should not continually be awakened. This disrupts the baby's schedule, and many times visitors come with a wide assortment of germs. The result is a sick, cranky baby.

The First Year

Feeding

As we have mentioned before, the first two weeks should be either breast or formula feedings; that's it. Beginning at two weeks of age and for the next two weeks, the baby should be started on rice cereal, along with the breast milk or formula. The cereal should be given once in the morning and once in the evening before the milk is given in order for the baby to take as much cereal as possible. Begin with one tablespoon of dried rice cereal mixed with four tablespoons of milk. As the baby becomes older, he may want this recipe thicker. Simply reduce the milk. This may be either breast milk or formula. All solid foods should be fed with a spoon. Following each feeding of cereal, as much milk as the baby wants should be given. During these two weeks the amount of solids should be increased as desired by the baby.

Beginning the second month, rice cereal should be continued for the next four weeks as before. Add a new fruit each week for the next four weeks, starting with peaches, apple sauce, bananas, and pears. Again, these solids should be increased as desired, but they should not be mixed in the same bowl as the rice cereal. We want your baby to experience each food separately. The cereal and new fruit should be given once in the morning and again in the evening.

During the third month, you will notice that he is having an increase in appetite. This means he is ready for three meals of solid food feedings a day. For breakfast, any cereal may be given along with any fruit, always followed by the milk (not more than five ounces of formula). The noon meal will consist of vegetables, fruits and milk (not more than five ounces of formula). The vegetables consist of green beans the first week, squash the second, peas the third, and carrots the fourth week. In the evening, vegetables, fruits and milk should be given (not more than five ounces of formula). At bedtime, only milk is given. Not more than twenty ounces of formula per day should be given to your baby, including the milk on the cereal. Of course, it is not possible for you to measure breast milk, unless you pump your breast. However, the key is to make sure your baby gets plenty of solid foods and does not fill up on the milk.

The milk should be given only after the solid foods have been eaten. If the baby will not take the vegetables, then put all food and milk away and wait thirty minutes and try the vegetables again. After the baby has finished the amount of food placed on his plate, and if the baby is still hungry, then increase the solid foods, not the milk. Your baby has now been well fed for three complete months.

More solid foods (the second foods) are started at the beginning of the fourth month. For breakfast only the cereal and the fruits are given. For lunch, meat and vegetable combinations are given with the cereal. Chicken or ham can be used as the meat combined with a vegetable. For the evening meal, the meat and vegetable combinations are given again along with fruits. As you can see, we are giving the cereal two times daily, fruits two times daily, and the meat and vegetable combinations two times daily. Babies usually do not like the meat flavor, but this is the disadvantage of being a baby; they need to eat it anyway. Increase the solid foods if the baby is still hungry, but do not increase the milk consumption (no more than twenty ounces of formula per day).

The fifth month will continue much like the fourth. In addition, we add orange juice each morning (four ounces of juice mixed with four ounces of water). This combination does not have to be given all at once. It can be given at any time with the exception of one hour prior to feeding the solid foods. If the baby is not allergic to the orange juice, then you may try all juices; giving a new juice each week. In addition to this, you may start Jell-o, custards, and puddings. The purpose of this is obviously not the food content, but rather it enables the baby to begin chewing and to learn to eat something cold. These should be given as desserts for lunch and dinner in the amount of two teaspoons at each meal.

The sixth month will be the same as the fifth for breakfast and lunch. At the evening meal you should give your baby straight meats and straight vegetables (no longer the combination). You do this in order for your baby to learn the taste of the meat flavor. The rest of the solid foods remain the same. You need to increase the amounts of cereals, fruits, and vegetables each week. Also during this month, you need to introduce the cup. Use a regular plastic cup, and start by giving one ounce out of the cup and finishing with either the breast or the bottle. Over the next several months you will increase the amount of milk from the cup and decrease the milk from the breast or bottle. By twelve months, the baby will be off the bottle without any difficulty because of the gradual nature of this method. Also during this month, babies who are feeding by formula will need a change of milk. At this time, you should switch the formula to two-percent or sweet acidophilus milk. Babies tolerate these milks well, and they are much less expensive than the formula. However, certain vitamins do need to be added when this change is made. I recommend one dropper full daily of Vi-Dalyn or Poly-Vi-Sol with iron.

Your baby is now six months old. As you begin this seventh month, you will continue with all the solid foods three times a day. Increase the amount from the cup and decrease the amount taken from the bottle. You need to keep giving the juices as well.

During the eighth month, you should change from the second foods to the third foods. These have larger lumps, and the baby may hesitate for a feeding or two, but will very soon take them without any difficulty. The babies should remain on the third foods until one year of age.

At one year of age, you should introduce table food for breakfast and dinner and remain on the third foods for the noon feeding. This provides a well-balanced diet for the baby. All table food should be cut into small bites, and a small amount should be placed on the plate. Add more as the baby continues to eat. Don't force the child to eat in order to make him a member of the clean plate club. You will notice that at one year of age, the child's appetite will slightly decrease for two to three months. Then it will pick back up until two years of age. At this point, it will drop dramatically. In some cases you will be doing well to get your child to eat one meal every two days. This will last for approximately six months. Don't force the child to eat. Always remember, the child will eat when he gets hungry.

SUMMARY

Month 1	**First two weeks:** breast or bottle (Similac) feedings every four hours in the daytime.
	Second two weeks: Rice cereal twice a day with milk every four hours in the daytime.
Month 2	Cereal and fruit twice daily with milk every four hours during the daytime.
Month 3	**Second foods**
	Breakfast: Cereals, fruits, and breast or formula (five ounces)
	Lunch: Vegetables, fruits, and breast or formula (five ounces)
	Dinner: Vegetables, cereals, and breast or formula (five ounces)
	Bedtime: Breast or formula (five ounces)

Month 4	**Breakfast:** Cereals and fruits, and breast or formula (five ounces) **Lunch:** Combined meats and vegetables with cereal, and breast or formula (five ounces) **Dinner:** Combined meats and vegetables with fruits, and breast or formula (five ounces) **Bedtime:** Breast or formula (five ounces)
Month 5	Same as month 4, but add juices, Jell-o, and custards
Month 6	Same as month 5, but give the straight meats and vegetables. Add the cup and exchange formula for two-percent or sweet acidophilus milk.
Month 7	Same as month 6.
Month 8	Change from the second foods to the third foods.
Months 9-12	Same as Month 8
1 year	**Breakfast and Dinner:** Change from third foods to table foods. **Lunch:** Continue with the third foods for two to three months or until the child refuses the third foods, then go to all table foods.

A Note about Solid Foods

Regardless of whether you are breast or bottle feeding, solid food feedings should begin at two weeks of age. This raises a very large controversy in the field of Pediatrics. After forty-three years of seeing babies and treating my third generation of children, I am convinced that giving solid foods at an early age is the best method for both the baby and the mother.

I am asked frequently, "Can babies tolerate solid foods?" My firm answer is, "Yes!" When only milk is given for the first six weeks, the milk passes through the digestive tract rather quickly and the result is a hungry baby. This in turn leaves a crying baby at all hours. The baby becomes anemic if he continues with just milk because it is low in iron. With the solid foods, there is more substance in the child's stomach and therefore the hunger pains do not occur as often. If you were hungry, would you be satisfied with a glass of ice tea, or a Thanksgiving feast? This method produces a baby that sleeps longer and appears more content. I have noticed no problems that develop from the use of this method and endorse it wholeheartedly.

The question usually arises concerning allergies to the solid foods. Now this does not take much thought and reason. With breast feeding, everything a mother takes in her stomach is passed directly through the breast milk. Most mothers are unlimited when it comes to their diet; however, if the child is allergic to something and the mother eats that, he will develop an allergy from the breast feeding at that time. Breast milk is fine to take, but a mother should not base her decision to breast feed on the false principle that solid foods cause more allergies.

When a baby has been on the bottle for two weeks with no allergy, proceed with solid foods. Each solid food is given for a week at a time to allow for any allergic reaction to occur. The reaction may be in the form of diarrhea, vomiting, or a skin rash. If a reaction of this sort occurs, make note of it. Later on, for instance, if a baby develops constipation, don't run out and get a laxative. Pull your notes out and give the baby a food that gave him diarrhea. This will solve his constipation problem. I would much rather use these natural foods to treat the child's symptoms than treat with medication.

The advantages of giving a baby solid foods early are simple. He sleeps all night by approximately two weeks of age, he is more content and satisfied, and his muscle tone is much firmer, not to mention the benefit of a mom's and dad's ability to sleep all night as well.

Sleeping

We have already mentioned that a baby should be placed in his own bed, with a firm mattress, in his own room, with the light out. It is not necessary to put a sheet or blanket over the baby because the child will more than likely kick it off. Instead, use pajamas that enclose the feet, and this will keep the baby sufficiently warm during the night. I would recommend that some sort of wedge be used to keep the baby on his side while he sleeps. There is a fear that a child who sleeps on his stomach has a higher risk of S.I.D.S. (Sudden Infant Death Syndrome). A baby who sleeps on his back has a higher risk of aspirating in the event that the child vomits during his sleep.

I would also alternate each end of the bed where the baby's head is placed. This keeps the head from deforming due to constantly sleeping on the same side.

Questions often arise as to the length of time a child should stay in a crib. When a child puts his leg over the side of his bed, this should be the day you get him a regular bed. At this time he is able to fall and do serious damage. This usually occurs around two years of age.

~

I hope this gives you some basic guidelines for the first year. Remember, these are general techniques and they are written for the average baby. Your baby is unique and special. Not all children will fit the mold. That is okay. As always, if you have any questions or any variance, especially dealing with the illnesses, make sure to consult your pediatrician.

Chapter 9

What Do I Do When... ? (Childhood)

You shall teach them diligently to your children,
and shall talk of them when you sit in your house,
when you walk by the way,
when you lie down,
and when you rise up.

DEUTERONOMY 6:7

I hope, the previous chapter was extremely informative to you. It is my intention that this chapter will be more of the same. While the previous chapter focused on the care of infants, this chapter will direct your attention to children between the ages of one and twelve. Again, we will focus on the discipline or training of the child. I hope both basic care and questions of discipline problems will be addressed to your satisfaction. This chapter as well as the previous is written to be a resource for you to refer to as you see these issues develop in your child. Again, I want to say that these solutions are tried and proven. They work; I promise.

Basic Care

Pacifier

Children who are still on the pacifier at eighteen months of age should have it removed. Continued use of the pacifier could lead to a deformity of the teeth and gums. A very simple way to eliminate the use of the pacifier is to cut the end off the nipple and then give the pacifier back to your child. If he continues to use it, then cut off more until your child throws it away by himself. It is much better for your child to throw the pacifier away himself, on his own, than for you to take it away from him.

Thumb Sucking

Thumb sucking is another bad habit that needs to be stopped by eighteen months of age. If you refuse, it will lead to a large dental bill later on. To break this habit, I have had good results using a solution called "Thum." You should paint the thumb with this solution several times daily, particularly at naptime or bedtime. While applying the solution, continue to inform the child that if he puts his thumb in his mouth, it will burn. Once again, we are explaining to the child the penalty for improper behavior. Most children will wait for one or two days, and then they will see if mother is telling them the truth. When the thumb goes in, the mouth will begin to burn. While it is burning, reapply more "Thum." Continue to do this for a week and the thumb sucking will usually be over. Some parents are concerned about the child's getting the solution in the eyes. I have never had this to happen.

Now, my granddaughter, Mary Grace, was a BIG thumbsucker. She also seemed to develop an unusual acquired taste for "Thum." Her mommy took a Band-aid and placed it on her thumb and referred to it as her boo-boo. Mary Grace did not want to suck on the Band-aid, but she also liked the attention she got from her boo-boo. Almost immediately, she stopped sucking her thumb. After a couple of weeks, she stopped using the Band-aid and never sucked her thumb again.

Potty Training

Within the realm of parenting, there are quite a number of tasks that you are responsible to complete. Some of these are rather routine, with easy instructions to follow. Others are more difficult, demanding a great deal of discretion on the part of the parents. Potty training is unfortunately connected with this second scenario. The good news: There are instructions. The bad news: They require a lot of patience on your part.

Generally, I suggest you first attempt potty training when your child reaches eighteen months of age. Now this by no means indicates that every eighteen-month-old is ready. Yet some are, and if your child is, this is a good time to try. If your child is pulling at his diaper or getting his own diaper for you to change him, you need to begin the training process.

Let me say, first and foremost, never use punishment or force in attempting to potty train your child. It will not work, and you are digging yourself a hole that will take a long time to climb out of. You start training by taking the child after each meal to the potty. Try putting him on the big potty first. You may want to turn him around backwards so he will not feel like they are falling, and this will give him something to hold on to as well. If your child likes the big potty, that is fine, but if not, try the little potty on the floor. We start with the big one because a chld sees Mom and Dad using it, and he wants to imitate them. If the child is unhappy or begins to cry, then remove him at once. If the child doesn't seem to mind it, leave him there about ten minutes. You may consider reading to him or even playing music. If he succeeds and goes to the potty at the right time, throw a party and reward him for his accomplishments. If he doesn't, then get him down and don't say anything about it.

Now, if at eighteen months your child wants to do this, fine. If he wants to do it for a week and then decides he doesn't want to be potty trained anymore and wants to stop, then you stop. If he is not interested at all, then wait another month and then try the same process

This is one thing you cannot force your child to do.

again. Don't ever ask him, "Do you want to go to the bathroom?" He will always answer, "No." As you and he are walking down the hall, lead him into the bathroom. If he doesn't say anything, put him on the potty. But if, when you turn in the bathroom, he says he doesn't want to go, back off. This is one thing you cannot force your child to do. He has full control, and he will do it when he gets ready. You can rest assured in the fact that all children at some point will be trained, even though you don't think they will.

If you are training during the warm months of the year, then place the child in very thin undergarments and put him outside. If the child plays all day and never comes in the house, then he is obviously not ready to be potty trained. If, however, he does have an accident and then comes in to be changed, delay the changing for a few minutes. It gives him a few minutes to consider what he has done and lets him realize that this would not have happened if he had just come in a few minutes earlier. Yet, you do not ever force or punish your child in any of these situations.

Also, you never let the child know that you want him to be potty trained. When you punish him for other wrongdoings, if he knows that Mom really wants him to be potty trained, he will mess in his pants in order to get you back for punishing him. Then you will not be able to do anything. You become angry. That is exactly what he wants to see. He is getting you mad for what you did to him. Therefore, never let him know that you want him to be trained.

One of my four-year-old patients went to Monteagle on a family vacation. They had a delightful time, but when it was time to return, the little girl did not want to leave. The mother explained to her that they had to return because Daddy had to get back to work. So they got in the car and about half way back she leaned over the seat and informed her mother that she was going to start messing in her pants again. Now this would have infuriated most mothers, and they would have disciplined their child for sarcasm. But this wise mother responded, "Fine, if that is what you want to do, then do it."

For one week, the child stopped being trained. The mother never let on that she was hurt or disappointed. She continued to change her as if she were a baby. And after a week had gone by, the little girl said to her mom, "Well, you don't seem to be getting mad at me, so I am going to go back to being potty trained." Now if the mother had gotten upset at first, then the child's defiance could have continued for a long period of time.

Smoking

Smoking should NEVER be done in the home or in the car with your children. This goes doubly so for newborn babies. Secondhand smoke has SEVERE adverse effects on babies as well as older children. On top of all that, what kind of example do you want to be setting for your children? They are your top priority.

Teeth Care and the Dentist

At approximately two years of age, a child should begin to brush his teeth. Always let the child do it himself. You may want to help guide his hand, but don't brush them for him. Some children will want to do it before age two and that is fine, if he initiates it. No special toothpaste is needed at this age unless dental problems are already present.

I would recommend that a child's first trip to the dentist should be between the ages of four and five. Of course, some children have dental troubles that dictate a trip to the dentist earlier than four or five.

How to Get Your Children to Eat Their Veggies

"Okay that's it! I told you to eat your vegetables! I'm going to get the timer. No dessert for you tonight!" Does this sound familiar? One child remembers this saga:

The one that I hated the most was the timer. It was never a clock. It had to be the little wind-up buzzer mother used for baking cakes. You could hear it tick for every second of your agony as you stared at your veggies, now cold from delay. You contemplated for what seemed to be hours just how you could dispose of these horrible excuses for food, without them entering your digestive tract. There was the dog, the potty, the trash can. Now how can I divert Mom's attention? All of a sudden, the buzzer goes off. Now you have had it!

Would you like to have a sensible and easy solution to this problem? Well here it is. If your child refuses to eat his vegetables at lunch, no problem. Just wrap them up and put them back in the refrigerator. Make sure that he does not get any other food until dinner. Then for dinner, reheat the vegetables and serve only those to your child.

He will have reached the point where hunger outweighs taste buds.

He will probably turn up his nose again. That's fine. Guess what he is having for breakfast? For the morning meal, out pops those vegetables. Your child will begin to realize you are not going to give in. At some point, maybe lunch, maybe dinner, maybe even breakfast the following morning, your child will gobble up those vegetables as fast as he can. He will have reached the point where hunger outweighs taste buds. The next time, he will not be nearly so defiant.

Discipline is needed in establishing good eating habits. This is a harmless way for you to win the battle. Mothers, just as a word of consolation: No child has ever died of starvation when good food is lovingly placed in front of him. Let me give you an extreme example of this.

A four-year-old child was brought into my office on a Monday morning and appeared extremely anemic. To my shock, the parents informed me that the child had in the past four years had nothing to eat but milk. In disbelief, I said, "Nothing?" The father spoke up and said, "Now, honey, there was that one time when he had a bite of ice cream." The parents were not joking. This child had eaten nothing but milk for the first four years of his life. I asked them why. They said that he just preferred milk, and they obliged.

Immediately, I put the child in the hospital with the orders that he could have anything to eat, except milk. From Monday until Friday, the child ate absolutely nothing. However, on Friday morning, that child dove into his plate full of food and ate every scrap he could find.

A child's choice of food is an expression of his will. He is asserting his sinful nature by satisfying his fleshly desires. God gave the child to parents in order for the parents to give him what he needs, not just what he wants.

Illnesses

Fever

The normal temperature for an average baby is the same as for an adult, 98.6°. Some children, just like adults, may run a degree above this or below all the time, but 98.6° is the average. Before the age of three, a baby's temperature should be taken rectally. Make sure to hold the thermometer while taking the child's temperature. This is a very good way to get an accurate reading. The temperature can also be taken under the child's arm. This is a less accurate way and a degree usually has to be added to the reading. I would not suggest the gadgets that read the child's temperature through the ear or patches on the forehead. These, while fine for adults, do not generate accurate readings in children.

The following guidelines will help you in knowing what to do when your child runs a fever. This breakdown is to be used for normal children with no other symptoms but a fever.

98.7° to 100°   Don't do anything except give extra fluids.

100.5° to 102.5° This is characterized as a low-grade fever. Tempra or Tylenol in a child's dosage should be given to the child to help reduce the fever. No aspirin should be given. If this low-grade fever persists for longer than twenty-four hours you should consult your pediatrician.

102.5° & above   Contact your pediatrician.

Diarrhea

In the event that a child past infancy gets diarrhea, you should begin by taking your child off all milk, juices, and solid foods for a period of twenty-four hours. Give carbonated drinks, tea, water, Gatorade, or any other beverage that is not milk or juice. Kaopectate is also very effective for diarrhea. If this problem persists longer than twenty-four hours, or if blood is seen in the stool, you should contact your pediatrician.

Constipation

I prefer to handle constipation with diet alone. Remember that I told you during the first year to write down and keep track of those foods that caused your child to have diarrhea. This is so that later in life, when your child develops constipation, those foods can be used instead of over-the-counter medications. Things such as prune juice, green vegetables, and apple juice cause diarrhea in many children, and these are what I would use to treat constipation in your child. This will work in most all cases and serves as another advantage of starting your children on solid foods as soon as possible.

If the constipation is acute (sudden), or if it persists for twenty-four to forty-eight hours, you might try glycerin suppositories. If this problem persists, consult with your pediatrician.

Ear Infections

These are extremely common in young children. In adult ears, the eustachian tube, that runs from the inner ear to the throat, is large enough to successfully drain the middle ear. In small children, this eustachian tube is not large enough to always do the job. It often gets stopped up, which causes pain and infections.

These infections are usually treated with antibiotics prescribed by your pediatrician. In the past, ventilation tubes were often used, but it was found that a greater percentage of children who used these tubes were developing permanent deafness later on in life. Now these tubes are prescribed for patients who have severe ear problems and can't get over these infections with the use of antibiotics.

Indications or symptoms that your child has an ear infection may be things such as your child's pulling at his ear or if old enough, he will simply tell you that his ear hurts. He may place his ear close to you, enjoying the warmth against the ear. Oftentimes a fever or vomiting will accompany an ear infection. Again, if any of these are detected, you need to call your pediatrician immediately.

Cuts and Scrapes

For most basic cuts and scrapes a simple bandage placed over the injury should be used, and it is recommended to put some type of antiseptic on the injury before the bandage is placed. At night, it is best to remove the bandage to allow fresh air to get to the wound for quicker healing.

Occasionally, in a more serious injury, the skin edges will be pulled apart and hang open. This is usually a good indication that sutures will be required. Pressure should be placed on the injury and the child should immediately be taken to a physician.

If a cut or scrape ever begins to produce a greenish-yellow drainage, indicating an infection, you should contact your pediatrician.

Burns

There are three classifications for burns, each requiring different degrees of treatment. The following classifications are a recommended procedure.

First-degree burn: This is similar to a bad sunburn. Usually some type of spray to relieve the pain is adequate along with some Calladryll lotion to eliminate itching.

Second-degree burn: This is a more serious burn that would form a blister of any size. It is important not to rupture this blister consciously. If it ruptures on its own, you are not to worry. When the injury first occurs, cold water or butter help take some of the immediate pain away. If a blister of any size forms, you should contact your pediatrician.

Third-degree burn: This is the most serious of burns and is detected if a burn is deep enough to reveal muscle. In the event of this injury, you should cover the area with a clean, wet cloth. Stay away from all ointments and lotions and rush the child immediately to the emergency room for further treatment.

Skin Rash

Most skin rashes will be either allergic or dermatitis. An ointment such as Neosporin should be applied three times a day. Caladryl lotion may be used to reduce itching.

In some cases, a fever will accompany the rash. If this is the case, you need to contact your pediatrician.

Common Cold

If symptoms of a common cold develop, you don't need to panic. If a sore throat begins, you may use throat lozenges, and if the child is old enough, he may gargle with warm salt water. A cool mist humidifier is also a good treatment to place in the child's room at night. Make sure to clean the humidifier very well before each use to eliminate any bacteria that may be spread into the air.

There are a number of conditions that may persist that would warrant a call to the pediatrician. If the cold lasts for longer than forty-eight to seventy-two hours, if a fever over 100.5° lasts for twenty-four hours, or if a sore throat persists for more than forty-eight hours, you should make that call to your pediatrician.

Seizures/Convulsions

Most seizures occur because of a high fever. Some things you can do immediately to help reduce the fever is to scrub the child with a mixture of one-half room-temperature water and one-half rubbing alcohol using a washcloth. Scrub intensely turning the skin red. This helps lower the temperature by bringing the blood vessels closer to the skin. Do not use cold water because this tends to increase the fever.

One concern during a seizure is the child's swallowing his tongue. Do not put your fingers in the mouth of a convulsing child. There is a good chance you will get bitten, sometimes rather badly. Instead, place a spoon or pen in the mouth and then grab for the tongue. This keeps you from getting bitten.

In the event of any seizure or convulsion, leave the child on the floor and call your pediatrician immediately.

Other Reasons for Calling Your Pediatrician

In addition to those already mentioned . . .
* If your baby has a stiff neck.
* Failure to urinate every eight hours.
* A drastic decrease in eating habits.
* Rapid breathing.
* Blue color, especially around the mouth.
* Vomiting or bloody diarrhea.
* Difficulty in awakening the child.
* External bleeding from any site.

There are many other conditions that would warrant a call to your pediatrician. These mentioned are signs that require immediate attention. Don't hesitate to call your pediatrician at any time if you suspect something to be abnormal in your child.

Materials to Have Ready When Calling a Doctor

* Give name of parent and child; don't expect your pediatrician to remember you.
* Age of child
* Length of illness
* Temperature
* Rashes associated with illness
* Occurrences of diarrhea or vomiting
* Status on eating
* Any allergies
* Status on bowel movements and urination

Preparing for ...
Bed, School, Church, and Sibling Rivalry

How to Get Your Kids to Go to Bed

"Johnny, go take your bath," commands his mom ever so politely. Johnny continues to stare at the television. "Johnny, I said, go take your bath!" demands his mom, this time with increased volume and tone. Johnny appears as though he has heard nothing. Then, finally, the shrill, the horrific scream, "Johnny, GO TAKE YOUR BATH!!!!!!!!" This time Johnny jumps as though he has been shot and runs to the bath-room.

Why can't a lower frequency achieve the same results? Why should Johnny's mom have to reach this point? I propose that she doesn't. What is an effective way to get Johnny's attention? Try the count-ing method. You start by asking in a calm unexcitable voice, "Johnny, go take your bath." If Johnny pre-tends not to hear, begin to count. It is a simple one-two-three. You are in control. You may count slowly or fast, but if "three" is reached, pun-ishment is followed. The only prerequisite to this method is that you explain this procedure to Johnny at a time when you have his full atten-tion.

> *"All children are angels,*
> *and every house is heaven*
> *when they are asleep."*

My wife, Betty, used this method the first time with her grand-daughter, Mary Grace. Coincidentally, Mary Grace had just learned to count. My wife slowly began to count one, two—and Mary Grace fin-ished hurriedly three, four, five, six, seven, eight, nine, ten. Both laughed hysterically. This can happen when you fail to explain the procedure. This explanation should not come in the heat of the moment. When the conflict arises, the understanding of the rules must already be in place.

Use the counting method, and achieve the difficult daily task of bedtime. No more screaming, no more yelling, no more shrieking, no more crying. That sounds pretty good, doesn't it? Imogene Fey once said, "All children are angels, and every house is heaven when they are asleep."[1]

How to Prepare Your Child for School

When your child reaches three to three-and-a-half years of age, it is time to begin preparing him for the school experience. At this age, you may begin taking your child to a quality day care for a half day about twice a week. It is vitally important that you pick your child up and be

> *I would be very fearful to leave my child in a setting where discipline was not enforced and world-views were anti-Christian.*

on time. This way your child will learn that Mom leaves him, but he can be sure she will pick him up. At this age, it is also important that mother and child experience some time of separation. Consequently, kindergarten will not be such a severe shock.

The type of day care that you send your child to is very important. Love your child enough not to leave him with just any institution with a license. Personally go to the day care and investigate its treatment of the children. I would be very fearful to leave my child in a setting where discipline was not enforced and world views were anti-Christian.

This same concern for your child's treatment and education should not stop at day care. There are many great public schools; there are many bad public schools. There are many great private schools; there are many bad private schools. There are many great homeschool environments; there are many bad homeschool environments. I say that to say this: All three types of education are potentially good. It is up to you to investigate which one would be most beneficial for your child, in your unique situation. No one particular way is right.

I will give just a word of instruction concerning homeschooling. I think that if public or private schools are acceptable where you live, then they should be utilized unless the Lord tells you otherwise. Don't keep your child home just to be with him more. However, if the conditions of the schools are unacceptable, and you sense God directing you to homeschool, I would strongly urge you to give your child multiple kinds of interaction with other children. This is vital to their social orientation later in life. I am in awe of parents who because of a desire to put their children first, forsake their own personal time, and sacrifice several years of their lives in order to provide a Biblically sound education for their children in the format of homeschooling. If you do this, you are to be commended.

How to Prepare Your Child for Church

One little boy said to his mom, "Can I be a preacher when I grow up?" "Why, certainly you may," said his proud mother. "But I didn't know you enjoyed church so much." "I don't," Johnny said, "but as long as I have to go there for the rest of my life anyway, I'd rather do the shouting than the sitting."

One rather disconcerting aspect of parenting is knowing how to properly prepare your children for the worship experience. When do I take them to "big church?" How do I get them to sit still for an hour? In what ways can I make church more meaningful to my child? How do I encourage my child's decision for Christ in a way that will not force him to believe like Mom and Dad?

So many questions; now it's time for some answers. Before your child's fourth birthday, it is my suggestion that you utilize the church nursery, if indeed your church has one. Before the age of four, your child will reap very little from the "big worship service." However, a dynamic children's program can be very instrumental in teaching your child some basics about God during these years. Prior to four years of age, you will find it frustrating for you, your child, and those around you, if you try to bring him into the service. He *WILL* be disruptive. You can count on it. Use the nursery; that is why it is there.

Just a note about the nursery: When you first begin to take your child to the nursery, make sure you are there to pick him up, just like in day care. Let him see your face, don't send somebody else. Also, you will want to be on time. This will build within your child a trust for you. You were where you were supposed to be when you were supposed to be there.

Try your best to make church a positive experience.

When your child reaches the age of four, the preparation for worship can begin. Your child now has the capability of sitting for extended periods of time, as well as a developing curiosity about spiritual things. You will want to begin to take your child to the "big service" at intervals. I suggest the summer of his fourth year to take him on certain

Wednesday and Sunday nights. Then in the fall, a regular attendance pattern should be implemented. However, there is much preparation that can be done leading up to this time, and it will most certainly prove to be beneficial.

It is a given that children will try to imitate their parents. Your attitude about church will surely transfer to your child. Try your best to make church a positive experience. Confer to your child that "big church" is a privilege reserved for four-year-olds and above. This will build in your child an expectancy and anticipation for this new experience. If you want your child to make church a priority, you must model that in your own habits. Regular attendance is vitally important.

Part of training your child lies in setting the standards. It is important to establish rules for church, and it is essential that your child understands them. Explain to him that church is a time when the pastor tells us what God has to say. Therefore, we must listen very carefully and be very quiet so that we will not disturb others. Emphasize that this is the highlight of the week and demands our best behavior. Another rule you will want to make is that your child participate in the service. When the congregation stands, so should your child. When someone is praying, teach him to bow his head and close his eyes.

Now understand, especially when your child is young, that he may experience times of restlessness. Remember that he has never had to sit this long and be this quiet ever before. You may want to have toys available when necessary to distract his attention on these fidgety days. Sitting still often induces sleep in children. This is fine. Before the service begins, it is good to take your child to the bathroom and let him get a drink of water. This will keep you from having to do these things once the service begins.

Make sure that everyone is well rested before Sunday morning. If a child is tired, he tends to be more restless and disobedient. In our family, we would usually spend Saturday nights at home. This would allow for us to get plenty of sleep and be ready for Sunday morning.

Invariably you will have some very bad days—days that call for discipline. If your child begins to cry, take him out IMMEDIATELY!!! Don't wait and try to get him to stop. You want to eliminate the noise factor as quickly as possible. Make sure to enforce whatever penalty you have set with your child for church disobedience. Once that has been administered and the child has calmed down, slip back into the service. You never want to just go home, or your child will get the message that misbehavior is a quick passport to get out of church and on his way home.

Overall, this new experience can be wonderful. Your child will have many questions, all beginning with "Why does . . . ?" God is not someone we worship just on Sundays, but every day of the week. Therefore, it is essential that you teach your child spiritual things during the week. Sing songs around the house, pray with him before he goes to sleep, reinforce what was taught to him on Sunday, and have family devotions. All of this will build within your child priceless truths that he will bear in his conscience all the days of his life.

How to Handle Sibling Rivalry

A young girl asked her older brother if she had been adopted. He replied, "Yes, but they brought you back."

Children will often clash. The egos of siblings love to get on each other's nerves. From an outsider, it often looks as though they hate one another. They are competitive and conniving creatures out to win their way. Brothers and sisters—how does a parent get them to live at peace with one another?

Well, to answer that question simply is to say, "You can't." Their rivalry, however, is not always a bad thing. Through it, they learn how to operate with one another, they experience how to forgive, and they learn how to work and play together. These interactive skills will follow them throughout their life.

But how should a parent handle these situations? For the most part, I would allow the children to work out their conflicts on their own. Only when a house rule has been broken should the parents step in and discipline. I am referring to rules against hitting or calling each other bad names. These justify the parents' call to action.

It is wrong for the parents to always come to the rescue of the smaller child. It is often the baby in the family who is causing most of the problems. It also is inappropriate for the parent to approach the conflict trying to determine who is right. Often the best solution is found, not in who is right, but what is right. Let me explain. Both children will feel they are right. If you choose a side, the other child will take that as favoritism. So I encourage you to pick at the problem, not at the person.

Let me give you an example. You hear your older son and younger daughter screaming and yelling at one another. All of a sudden the daughter begins to cry. Off you go, stomping up the stairs, to ring the bell, ending the final round. Your first reaction is to ask what happened. You assess from their two Oscar-winning performances of explanation that the gist of the problem occurred because they began calling each other names, and this led to repeated hitting until the older boy hurt his younger sister.

Now a parent would be making an error if he tried to find out who started it. That is not important. They both are guilty of breaking the law. The law in this house calls for no hitting and no name calling. It doesn't matter who started it. Both should be punished because they both broke the law.

In cases of sibling rivalry, the parent needs to serve as an impartial judge. Try not to ever take sides. Let them both know that when Mom and Dad catch them in a fight that both are most likely to be punished. This will encourage their compatibility and lessen their competition because both are punished and there is no winner in their rivalry.

Can You Start Over?

I realize that some of you who are reading this book are already in the process of training children. You may be saying, "I wish I could start over and try this method on my child." Maybe you are in a situation where you have a child who is very disobedient and you feel as though you have lost control. You may be asking, "Is there any way I could start over?" I have some good news. While you can't start from day one, you can begin again from where you are now.

I have seen multiple examples of children who have had radical changes in their temperament because their parents cared enough and put forth the enormous effort to clean the slate of expectations and start anew and afresh. It can be done, but it takes dedication and determination.

Perhaps, one of the most drastic changes that I have witnessed occurred in a little girl named Jennifer. At four years of age, it would be appropriate to say that she ruled the household. She was conceivably the worst-behaved child that I have ever seen. She was

> *She wanted boundaries, and once they were given, she operated beautifully in accordance with them.*

extremely rude, talked back, and was out of control. She spent much of her time at her great-grandmother's house as well as her grandparents'. Every house she was in, she totally dominated. Her grandparents approached me about the child's constant back-talking and repeated hitting of her parents. She had to be the center of attention. They operated on the philosophy that just loving her would do the trick. This was the first grandchild, and discipline in their mind was not an option. They had reached the point of utter confusion and wanted to know if anything could be done.

I shared with them some of the techniques and principles you have read in this book. We brought in all of the authorities in this girl's life. We made sure that everyone was in agreement as to the changes that would have to be made if Jennifer were going to turn around. They all agreed and began to take control and set the standards.

Within forty-eight hours, Jennifer had made a 180-degree turn. She is now arguably one of the most polite children I know. Jennifer knew she was out of line. She was extremely bright and very aware of what was taking place. She wanted boundaries, and once they were given, she operated beautifully in accordance with them.

So to answer the question: You can start again. It takes unison among the child's authorities, firmness, openness, hard work, and patience, but it is well worth the effort.

Chapter 10

The Heritage of a Holy Home

Behold, children are a heritage from the LORD,
the fruit of the womb is a reward.
Like arrows in the hand of a warrior,
so are the children of one's youth.
Happy is the man who has his quiver full of them.

PSALM 127:3-5

A man and his little girl were in an elevator. Suddenly, a lady in front turned around, slapped the man, and left in a huff. The little girl remarked, "I'm glad she's gone. She stepped on my toe, so I pinched her."

Children are a fascinating creation of God. When you watch their antics and pranks, you cannot doubt the fact that God has a sense of humor. Much of this book has concerned itself with the negative behaviors of children and how to correct them. Every negative has a positive, and so it is with children.

This chapter is dedicated to highlight the blessings of children

> *God's sovereign control will ultimately see His plans for your child fulfilled.*

and their benefits to parents. It is designed to put you, the parent, at ease. While parenting can bring with it much consternation and many headaches, it will most certainly produce some of the best times life has to offer. While you play a huge part in the future performance of your child, you must not forget who is directing the play. God's sovereign control will ultimately see His plans for your child fulfilled. Parents are God's helpmates in raising children, not the determining factor. So relax; settle down; you don't have to be a perfect parent. You have a pretty good team member who will help you pick up the slack. Enjoy your children while you have them. They are truly a gift from God.

A Holy Heritage

Psalm 127:3 says, "Behold, children are a heritage from the LORD, the fruit of the womb is a reward." The word "heritage" carries with it the idea of a gift given to someone out of someone's property and possessions. The verb form of the word in Hebrew means giving an assignment to someone. Therefore, children are God's possessions that He assigns to parents to train them in the way they should go. The children belong to God and they always will. Parents simply have them on loan.

TO ALL PARENTS

"I'll lend you for a little time
A child of Mine," He said,
"For you to love the while he lives
And mourn for when he is dead.
It may be six or seven years,
Or twenty-two or three;
But will you, 'til I call him back,
Take care of him for Me?
He'll bring his charms to gladden you,
And should his stay be brief,
You'll have his loving memories
As solace for your grief.
I cannot promise he will stay,
Since all from earth return,
But there are lessons taught down there
I want this child to learn,
I've looked the wide world over
In My search for teachers true,
And from all the throngs that crowd
Life's lanes I've selected you.
Now will you give him all your love,
Not think the labor vain,
Nor hate Me when I come to call
To take him back again?
I fancied that I heard them say,
"Dear Lord, Thy will be done."
For all the joy Thy child shall bring,
The risk of grief we'll run.
We'll shelter him with tenderness,
We'll love him while we may.
And for the happiness we've known,
Forever grateful stay.
But should the angels call for him
Sooner than we've planned
We'll brave the bitter grief
That comes and try to understand.

— Edgar A. Guest[1]

Now folks, children belong to the Lord. They never become your possession. You manage, but you do not own. This is a nugget of truth that has been absent in the debate on abortion. Many women will say, "But it is my body, and I have the choice to do with my body that which I want." You are right. It is your body, but that which is in your body is God's, and you have no right to kill that which is His possession.

I want to say as a medical doctor in the field of pediatrics for over forty years that any kind of abortion at any stage in the pregnancy is nothing short of murder. The one exception I would make to this rule is when the mother's physical life is in jeopardy, and even then it is a decision that involves the death of one of two viable human lives. I would also like to go on record by saying that I do not know any of my colleagues, outside of the money-making abortion industry, who would deny the fact that the tissue developing inside the mother's womb is a viable, living, human being. Proponents of abortion say there is no medical proof of this. I completely and totally reject that statement. There is enough proof to fill a book larger than this one that confirms the fetus is a viable human life from conception. I would challenge the pro-abortion proponents to find one shred of medical evidence that concludes that this tissue is anything but a living human being.

It is disgusting to see human life so devalued. If you have had an abortion, there is forgiveness from God for those with a heart of repentance. I want to remind you again that we are all possessions of God, which makes us infinitely valuable. God entrusts these precious children into the hands of parents. These valuable bundles of potential are not ours, but they are our responsibility. We are responsible to protect, to love, to provide for, to train, and to teach.

> *These valuable bundles of potential are not ours, but they are our responsibility.*

Mom and Dad: The Professor and the Principal

Children arrive in this world with little information about it. They have no value system, no moral code of conduct, no knowledge to pass an academic test, and no way to know where they can obtain such information. They are blank slates ready to be written upon, lumps of clay eager to be molded.

Unfortunately, we live in a society today that is competing heavily for the minds of our children. It puts out seductive propaganda to lure their minds into the trap of believing just about anything it wants them to. It is more crucial today than ever before that we grasp the earliest moments in their lives to teach them everything we know to be true and right. Parents, this is your responsibility. It is not the government's, not the church's, not even the schoolhouse's obligation—it is yours, and yours alone.

> *It is more crucial today than ever before that we grasp the earliest moments in their lives to teach them everything we know to be true and right.*

Children will learn what they are taught. We cannot expect the desirable attitudes and behavior to appear if we as parents have not properly taught them. If it is desirable that our children become kind, appreciative, well-behaved, respectful, responsible, hardworking adults, then these qualities must be taught, NOT hoped for. The permissive philosophy has produced a generation of undisciplined, untrained, mentally lagging, rebellious teenagers.

Now, I can hear some of you saying, "But I don't feel qualified; I don't have a master's in education." One teacher said to her student, "I don't see how one person could make so many mistakes on his homework." The child responded, "It wasn't one person—my father helped me." You don't have to be a genius with all of the answers. It is the basics, the fundamentals of life, the values you hold to be strong and pure; these are the lessons of living that you must instill into your children. Why you? Because if you don't, someone else will.

Where to Teach

In my opinion, EVERY CHILD SHOULD BE HOME-

SCHOOLED!!! In case you didn't get it, I'll repeat it, ALL CHIL-
DREN NEED A HOMESCHOOLED EDUCATION! Now before
you close this book, let me explain what I mean.

> *"A child educated only at school is an uneducated child."*

I have already said in previous chapters that if quality private
or public schools are within your
resources then they should be utilized unless God says otherwise. So
you are probably wondering why I
just made this contradictory state-
ment in the above paragraph. Well, I am not necessarily referring to
formal education. But as George Santayana has well said, "A child educated only at school is an uneducated child."[2] William Temple states,
"The most influential of all educational factors is the conversation in a
child's home."[3] This is why I say that every child must be homeschooled
in addition to whatever formal education he receives.

Don't leave your child's education to the school system. I have
witnessed scores of people who are much smarter than I, whose values
and principles have been corrupted due to furthering their education.
Don't get the idea that your child will be rightly educated when he gets
a diploma in his hand, or if he comes home with all A's. I remind you
that almost every offender of Watergate was a graduate of an Ivy League
school such as Harvard University.[4]

Teach your child how to think and communicate with others.
Make your home a forum for exchanging ideas. Spend time at the dinner
table sharing opinions on varying subjects. Turn off the television and
help him expand his mind through deep conversation. Make sure that
by the time your child leaves your home that he knows fully your values
and principles, what you believe in, and what you would die for. These
skills will help him so very much when he reaches the real world, a world
that will pressure him to turn from traditional values and explore new
avenues. It is then that the rewards of labor that transpired within the
home will bear fruit for all eternity.

Iimagine the number of children that I have seen in the course
of almost forty years of Pediatrics. Few, however, touched my heart
like Stacey. This beautiful, sandy-haired, innocent little girl was diag-

nosed with leukemia when she was in her early teens. Unlike many of my patients, Stacey was old enough to communicate well with us. She was a loving and affectionate child. She was very outgoing. One nurse remarked that Stacey never met a stranger.

She spent much of her three years after diagnosis traveling to and from St. Jude's Children's Research Hospital in Memphis, Tennessee. While she was in Nashville, she would make her weekly visits to the office to receive her injections. She never complained and always had an upbeat personality. I almost felt as if she were my own child.

Stacey's affectionate personality was not surprising considering her family. She was their life. They loved Stacey, and would do anything for her. This love transferred to Stacey and then to everyone else she met.

Stacey's condition worsened. St. Jude's informed her parents that they had done all that they could do. The decision was left up to Stacey as to where she wanted to go. Her answer: "Home!" She wanted to spend her remaining days at home.

Our office staff had fallen in love with Stacey. There was not a day that went by that someone in the office did not make a house call. We did not charge any fee for this because the parents could not afford such personal care, yet Stacey demanded it from our hearts.

Week after week, day after day, we would go visit our special friend. Her room had been moved to the study where she could be in the center of activity. I would walk through the double French doors, across the hardwood floors over to Stacey's little bed on the right side of the room. There she would smile with her face buried in several fluffy pillows and her body lying in the midst of her bright white sheets and comforter. She was home. She was where she wanted to be.

Soon the phone call that I dreaded came from Stacey's father informing me that it wouldn't be long. I quickly rushed to the house and entered Stacey's room for the last time. I turned to her parents, now worn from the toll of a child with a terminal illness, and said, "She's gone." She was their life, their love, their little girl—and now she was gone.

As I reflect several years after Stacey's passing, I believe what I took away from this experience most was Stacey's resolve that she didn't want to die in a strange hospital bed in Memphis. She wanted to die at home. That is where love was, and love is who she was. Oh, how I pray that our homes would be havens of love.

I want to close this section with a word from Samuel Griswold Goodrich that encapsulates what I am trying to say:

> *The fireside is a seminary of infinite importance. Few can receive the honors of a college, but all are graduates of the home. The learning of the university may fade from the recollection, its classic lore may moulder in the halls of memory; but the simple lessons of home, enameled upon the heart of childhood, defy the rust of years, and outlive the more mature but less vivid pictures of after years.[5]*

When to Teach

The Bible tells us in Deuteronomy 6:4-7:

> *Hear, O Israel: The LORD our God, the LORD is one! You shall love the LORD your God with all your heart, with all your soul, and with all your strength.*
>
> *And these words which I command you today shall be in your heart. You shall teach them diligently to your children, and shall talk of them when you sit in your house, when you walk by the way, when you lie down, and when you rise up.*

God tells parents **when to teach** their children: "when you sit in your house, when you walk by the way, when you lie down and when you rise up." In summary, seize every opportunity you can find to teach them.

Children are going to observe your lives with great interest. The times you spend with them can and should be invaluable sources of education. You can provide what most classrooms cannot. You can give them on-the-job training. For instance, it is one thing to teach them from the Bible the story of the Good Samaritan, how a man showed compassion on one less fortunate. It is altogether different, however, to let that child see you have compassion upon others.

My wife will never forget a lesson of life taught to her by her father one Christmas Eve. They were driving through town on their way to deliver some Christmas packages to their friends and relatives. As they passed an elderly man worn from the troubles of life, cold from the winter air, and alone at a time of celebration, her father stopped the car. He jumped out and handed the man a twenty-dollar bill and wished him a Merry Christmas. A lesson in living, a course in compassion, a book in benevolence—it was a day when a moment would last in her memory for a lifetime.

Patrick Morley says in his book *I Surrender,* "Teaching our children is not a collection of clever homilies, but a lifestyle—thousands of individual impressions that shape the values and beliefs of our children."[6] It is making every moment meaningful, every circumstance count. The lessons they learn in this manner will far supersede textbooks and syllabi.

What to Teach

If I had the opportunity to instill one truth into every boy and girl on the face of the globe, it would be this: **Jesus loves me this I know, for the Bible tells me so.** If you don't teach your children anything else, make doubly sure that this powerful principle is inscribed upon the tablets of their hearts.

> *If I had the opportunity to instill one truth into every boy and girl on the face of the globe, it would be this: Jesus loves me this I know, for the Bible tells me so.*

Samuel Sava has said, "It's not better teachers, texts, or curricula that our children need most; it's better childhoods, and we will never see lasting school reform until we see parent reform."[7] You can do it! You can be the one who gives your child the education of a lifetime.

Giving A Godly Heritage

Now following our consistent painting scenario, I want to illustrate this last image for heritage. A heritage is something that is used to train future generations, not just the one child you are raising now. This is why I liken heritage to the easel. The easel is the structure, the support that will hold many more canvases that will be painted on by the artist. If you have a good solid easel, it will endure many creations of masterpieces. If you build a strong, godly heritage, you will see the byproduct of many generations living for their Creator.

While it is true that children are a heritage of God, it is your responsibility as parents to give them a godly heritage. Understand this, providing a godly heritage does not mean that you have to be the perfect parent in the ideal situation. Developing a godly heritage involves taking the resources God has entrusted you with and using them to instill godliness and holiness into your home.

While it is true that children are a heritage of God, parents, it is your responsibility to give them a godly heritage.

Many parents think that they are successful only if the following conditions apply: They need a healthy child to start with, they need to be able to afford everything the child wants, their home has to be functional and contain all the modern-day luxuries, and their child must be the brightest in the class. Then and only then do some parents sit back and say, "I did a good job." Unfortunately, this parent also hears these children blame their parents when the world crumbles around them. The new version of an old saying goes like this: "If at first you don't succeed, blame your parents."[8] This is not right!

It is so frustrating today when you examine many of the books on parenting. Some of them are just plain scary for parents to read. They say if you don't do this, your child will be an ax murderer. If you don't do this over here, he will grow up to be a homosexual. But if you do this and this and this at these specific time periods, your child may turn out okay. But if he doesn't, you must have forgotten to do this along the way. It is crazy, and, might I add, very disheartening for parents. What have these experts left out of the picture? GOD!!

When God is in control, things such as physical fitness, financial freedom, harmonious homes, and brilliant brains fade in their power over the child's future. The sad part is that most parents worry more about providing these elements than they do building about godliness into their homes.

Physical Fitness

I recall one of my patients who was very sick at birth. His physique was such that we could not determine whether he was a boy or a girl. We did not resolve this until he was tested genetically. This child was allergic to everything that we put in his digestive tract. The only thing we found that he did not react to was ginger ale. Now, one might think that no child could survive just on ginger ale. When God wants a child to live, he can survive on anything. I am here to say that for the first two years of this child's life, the only thing he had to digest was ginger ale. Recently, I was in a restaurant in Nashville and had the pleasure of being waited on by this very handsome man. He is now in his late twenties and has no obvious physical limitations.

Now, to contrast this, I have had some parents who are so careful to feed their children properly that they literally count the intake of calories and fat grams their children will consume. All the while, they are failing to instill godliness in the children. Is diet important? Absolutely. But what is most important? Parents are meticulously caring for the physical needs of the children, while the spiritual is put on a back burner. I am not saying to take the physical off the stove, just make doubly sure the spiritual is given the most heat and that it remains first priority.

Financial Freedom

Let's turn our attention just a moment to those parents who feel they have to provide for their child all the luxuries of life that they were never afforded in their upbringing.

The following appeared in *The New York Times Magazine* and was written by Dorothy Barclay:

> *Dr. Barbara Biber gave the specialists one of the biggest laughs of the meeting with her story of the middle-aged matron who had never tasted the white meat of chicken. It seems a worthy wife*

and mother was asked at a dinner party which she preferred, the white or the dark, and threw her host into confusion by saying she really didn't know.

"You see," she told him simply, "when I was a child, my father used to carve the chicken. He'd ask all the adults which they preferred, and of course they said the white meat. So I was always served dark. Now I'm married and my husband carves. He asks the children which they prefer and of course they say the white. And so I've never tasted the white meat of chicken."

The moral of her parable, Dr. Biber was quick to add, is: "Parents today, the older ones certainly and many of the younger ones too, represent a transitional generation. Under the circumstances," she said, "we must be forgiving of our own errors. We are trying to live a life with our children that we have never tasted."[9]

How true that is. Many mothers are working outside the home not because they have to, but because they want to provide the luxuries for their children that they never had when they were growing up. They are trying to give their children a life they have never lived. In many cases, it is having a negative effect. Children are growing up without a work ethic, and they expect everything to be handed to them on a silver platter.

It is understandable that you want your child to have the best. The best, however, may not be everything that he wants. The cost of raising a child to age eighteen is approximately $150,000. Now I know parents who would say, "My child didn't cost no $150,000!" But I also know parents who say, "I wish ours had only cost $150,000!" I have seen good and bad children come out of both extremes. The

The key is not what you give them from your checkbook, but what you give them from your "lifebook."

key is not what you give them from your checkbook, but what you give them from your "lifebook." What will you communicate to them from your heart that will give them the guidelines for surviving life?

It seems as though parents are trying so hard to give their children what they didn't have, but so few are giving them what they did have—a home built day by day with principles rooted in the Word of God and a faith secure in the Everlasting Father. No luxury that money can buy will replace the genuine need for a godly heritage.

Heavenly Home

Many parents think they are destined to fail at parenting because they do not have a functional family. In this day and age, we would be foolish to think that all parents are involved in households with one mother, one father, 2.5 children, and a dog. I realize that many mothers may be reading this book facing a life of single parenting. I don't want to scare you into thinking that you can't do it and that your child will be marred by the experience. Some of you may be facing a situation where your spouse may not be a Christian. You are fearful that your child will reap the habits of your unsaved spouse. All of these are legitimate fears and apprehensions. I want to exhort you to look to God. He is waiting to fill the void in your family. Your main responsibility, especially in these circumstances, is to provide for your children a godly heritage in the midst of the confusion that surrounds them. Trust God, it can be accomplished.

Is having a functional home important? You bet it is! Can you be a successful parent if your home is dysfunctional? You bet you can! The key in both is instilling godliness into your children. God can make a dysfunctional home functional and a functional home even better.

Brilliant Brains

> *Reward him when he gives his best, not when the world says he is best.*

The last area that I want to caution parents about is the realm of education. Many parents take great pride in their children's education, and they should. When a child is gifted in academics, he should be praised for his achievements. But not all children are academic geniuses.

One little boy asked his mom, after returning home from school, "Mother, what does 'apt' mean?" "Why, it means smart, quick to learn," said the mother. "Why do you ask?" "Oh, nothing much," responded the boy, "The teacher told me today I was apt to flunk."

Children vary. Some are smart and some are not. It's rather funny: Parents believe wholeheartedly in heredity when their child's report card is all A's.[10] Remember there can be only one valedictorian in a class. Does that mean that you have failed as a parent if yours is not number one? Absolutely not! What you should strive for is not being number one or a report card with all A's, but a child who sets his sights on performing to the best of his abilities. This is a child who will go places. This is a standard that all parents can set with their children. Reward him when he gives his best, not when the world says he is best.

Once again, we have a situation where many parents direct so much of their energy, yet feel so frustrated. The lesson of excellence is found in the Word of God. Part of leaving behind a godly heritage is making sure that your children fully understand the principles and standards of the Word. Parents' first job is to communicate Biblical principles to their children before academic ones. When the former concept is established in their minds and hearts, the latter becomes a much easier task.

In Summary

These four areas represent just a small variety of problems that occupy the minds and efforts of parents who are seeking the best for their children. Oftentimes, I think the devil uses these to distract parents from carrying out their primary responsibility—that being to provide for them a godly heritage, an inheritance more valuable than silver and gold. I want you to ponder these wise words written by Patrick Morley in his book *I Surrender:*

> *To be godly parents is no guarantee that your children will turn out right; that they will follow the Lord and lead happy, productive lives. But to be ungodly parents is a virtual guarantee that they will turn out wrong. And if you don't do your part and by God's grace they turn out right, you will have had little to do with it.[11]*

A Household of Faith

It is your choice what kind of heritage you leave your child. I fully believe that your decision in this matter is perhaps the most important choice you will ever make as a parent. Just as you lived out the heritage of your parents, your children will most definitely live out the heritage that you leave them.

In his Family Life Seminar book, *You and Your Family*, Dr. Tim LaHaye diagrams a most interesting chart that traces the legacy of two men, both from the eighteenth century. The first man is Dr. Jonathan Edwards. He was the great orator of God who led one of the mightiest religious revivals in America, known as the Great Awakening. The other man was a moonshiner and one given to wildly extravagant and gross self-indulgent expenditure, who went by the name of Max Jukes. Max Jukes had 1,026 descendants. Three hundred of these died prematurely, one hundred were sent to prison, one hundred-ninety were prostitutes, and one hundred were known drunks. Do you understand a little better when God says in Exodus 20:5, "For I, the LORD your God, am a jealous God, visiting the iniquity of the fathers upon the children to the third and fourth generations of those who hate Me." In contrast, out of Jonathan Edwards' seven hundred twenty-nine descendants, three hundred were preachers, sixty-five were college professors, thirteen were authors, three were congressmen, and one was vice president of the United States.[12]

Again I will say that the heritage your children receive is up to you. The lifestyle you live, the values you hold dear, and the principles that guide your life will impact the future of your children. Not only will that heritage affect your children, but it has the potential to affect your children's children to the third and fourth generation.

> *"No nation has ever prospered in which family life was not held sacred."*

Your family life has a recourse that goes far beyond the walls of your home. Your home's environment will serve as a testimony to all who come in contact with your family. Dean William Inge has well said, "No nation has ever prospered in which family life was not held sacred."[13] The strength of the family is not a new idea. Great leaders from past generations have heralded this concept with great passion. Here is just a small selection of what two very important and wise people have said about the prominence of the family.

The family has always been the cornerstone of American society. Our families nurture, preserve, and pass on to each succeeding generation the values we share and cherish, values that are the foundation for our freedoms. In the family we learn our first lessons of god and man, love and discipline, rights and responsibilities, human dignity and human frailty.

Our families give us daily examples of these lessons being put into practice. In raising and instructing our children, in providing personal and compassionate care for the elderly, in maintaining the spiritual strength of religious commitment among our people—in these and other ways, America's families make immeasurable contributions to America's well-being.

Today more than ever, it is essential that these contributions not be taken for granted and that each of us remembers that the strength of our families is vital to the strength of our nation.

— President Ronald Reagan[14]

John S. Bonnell reported in his article "Power of the Home" a judge's perspective on the need for strong families. This is what he had to say:

Judge Camille Kelley has spent more than twenty years in salvaging children from society's scrap heap. Out of her experiences with 45,000 children who were brought before her, she observed, "The child's richest heritage is a well-ordered home. If every child had such an opportunity, delinquency would fade from court records. There would be no need for juvenile courts and juvenile judges." Then she added sadly, "But all children do not live in houses and all houses are not homes." That is the painful truth.[15]

Building homes with holy heritages—what better roots can you give your children?

Starting Out on the Right Foot

The story is told of a woman who was married fifteen years and had fourteen children. She wrote a columnist and said, "Do you think I ought to write a book?" The columnist replied, "No, I think you ought to READ one!"

This is certainly not the only book available on parenting. A great host of people would disagree with the principles found on these pages. Most of these individuals have spent a great deal of time listening to the so-called wisdom of the liberal media concerning the dangers of disciplining children. I caution you to choose wisely the advice you let come into your ears. If a person is not wise enough to believe in God and submit to His Lordship, what makes you think he is wise enough to train your child in the way he should go?

> *If a person is not wise enough to believe in God and submit to His Lordship, what makes you think he is wise enough to train your child in the way he should go?*

The book of James in the Bible speaks of a wisdom that is from above and a wisdom that is not from above. I have tried my best to provide you with wisdom that is from above. The basic principles of parenting—setting the standard, love, authority, trust, and discipline—are themes that come straight out of the Word of God. Not only are they rooted in Scripture, but they are also tried and proven. Put very simply—they work. The only trouble is, even with all this new information, it leaves the job of training children just as hard as ever.

If I Could Do It Again

Unfortunately, when you are a grandparent you begin to feel as though you have a grip on parenting. The following list was compiled by

The Heritage of a Holy Home

Terry Williams in an article entitled "What I Would Have Done Differently." The complete list contains the thoughts of fifty parents on raising children. The question asked of them was, "If you had it to do all over again, what would you do differently?" Here are a few of my favorites.

- *Never let my child know that it is even within the realm of possibility to buy ice cream from an ice cream truck.*
  — Mother of a four-year-old ice cream fanatic

- *I'd work as hard on planning good times for my husband and myself as I do planning them for the children.*
  —An attorney and a mother of two

- *I would have spent more time with them when they were young. Although you have their bodies for eighteen years, they're really only yours mentally and emotionally for a short time. Now I feel cheated.*
  — Mother of two teenagers

- *I wouldn't have put so much energy into my career. After spending this time with my son, I've found our relationship is more important than a promotion.*
  — Recently unemployed executive mother of a five-year-old

- *I would have stored up their hugs and kisses and love like pressed flowers to savor now.*
  — Eighty-year-old great-grandmother[16]

One of my lifelong friends, Wilson Tate, was asked what he would do differently if he had the opportunity to start over. He gave a list of five things:

- *I would spend more time with my children.*

- *I would not tell them how to do everything. I would let them be creative and do it their way.*

- *I would build a series of little successes in their lives.*

- *I would be positive and not critical.*

- *I would open our home to their friends. They would always feel welcome in our home.*

These are wise words from a grandparent. It's a shame you can't be a grandparent first, and then a parent. I hope that if you are just beginning the parenting process you will let this advice soak into your being. It comes from experience. It comes from people who did what they thought was right at the time, but now that they have gazed at the full picture of life, they realize what they missed.

> *It's a shame you can't be a grandparent first, and then a parent.*

A Final Thought

Well, it is time to begin your journey into Christian parenting. You are equipped with God's way to train a child. But, there is one ingredient that we have not talked about yet. This is perhaps the most important thing you can do for your child. Fashioning a home, setting the standard, building trust, maintaining authority, loving unconditionally, and teaching faithfully are all very necessary. Yet if people do not pray, they are cutting off their support system that was designed by God to make these principles work. He desires to help you in the process. Remember, your children belong to Him, and He wants what is best for them.

So, I encourage you to pray for your children. Ask God to fill their hearts with an undying love for Him. Ask Him to keep their hearts pure and their hands clean. Ask Him for His guardian angels to wrap their arms around your children and to protect them all the days of their lives. Ask Him to put a hunger and thirst for righteousness within their hearts that pounds relentlessly for the pursuit of the truth. Ask Him to help you, as their guardian, to train and to teach them to fear the Lord and to sow seeds that will bear much fruit. Admit to Him your inability to function completely as you ought. Ask Him to help you parent in such a way that your children will grow in the admonition and strength of the Lord. If you ask Him, I can promise you, based on His Word, that He will hear, and that He will heed your call.

The Heritage of a Holy Home

Remember that children are a heritage of the Lord. The Lord is good and everything that surrounds Him is wonderful. Your children are a good and wonderful gift of God. They will become the defining marks of who and what you ultimately will be. Build memories that will last and moments that will linger. This is what a heritage is all about.

One of our family's dearest friends was the late Bob Benson. He, perhaps better than anyone I know, could communicate these defining moments and memories of life. One of my favorite stories that he used to tell is entitled "Laughter In The Walls."

I pass a lot of houses on my way home—
some pretty,
some expensive,
some inviting—
but my heart always skips a beat
when I turn down the road
and see my house nestled against the hill.
I guess I'm especially proud
of the house and the way it looks because
I drew the plans myself.
It started out large enough for us—
I even had a study—
two teenage boys now reside in there.
And it had a guest room—
my girl and nine dolls are now permanent guests.
It had a small room Peg
had hoped would be her sewing room—
the two boys swinging on the Dutch door
have claimed this room as their own.
So it really doesn't look now
as if I am much of an architect.
But it will get larger again—
one by one they will go away
to work,
to college,
to service,

to their own houses,
and then there will be room—
a guest room,
a study,
and a sewing room
for just the two of us.
But it won't be empty—
every corner
every room
every nick
in the coffee table
will be crowded with memories.
Memories of picnics,
parties, Christmases,
bedside vigils, summers,
fires, winters, going barefoot,
leaving for vacation, cats,
conversations, black eyes,
graduations, first dates,
ball games, arguments,
washing dishes, bicycles,
dogs, boat rides,
getting home from vacation,
meals, rabbits and
a thousand other things
that fill the lives
of those who would raise five.
And Peg and I will sit
quietly by the fire
and listen to the
laughter in the walls.[17]

Godmother of my precious grandchildren and my nurse for many years, Miss Ann has watched thousands of children grow before her eyes. She has seen these principles put to practice in countless numbers of our patients' homes. Her advice: "Take advantage of the time you have; it is gone so quickly. Most of us spend so much time on the insignificant, the valleys of our life, that we never get to experience the mountain tops. These discipline principles are not byproducts of a modern-day mentality. It is not Dr. Spock; it is the Bible. It is what is supposed to be done."

My final and best advice: Take your children to church, don't just send them. Pray for your children every day of your life. And finally, use the best knowledge that you have. You are held accountable only for that knowledge which you have, not someone else's. And when you have done all of this, then and only then can you rely on God's principle from Proverbs 22:6, "Train up a child in the way he should go, and when he is old, he will not depart from it."

Notes

Unless otherwise noted, the Scripture quotations in this publication are from *The Holy Bible, New King James Version*, © 1982. Other version cited as (NIV) is taken from the *Holy Bible: New International Version*, © 1984 by the International Bible Society.

Chapter 1: "First Things First"

1. James Dobson, *Dare To Discipline* (Wheaton, Illinois: Tyndale House Publishers, Inc., 1970), 20.
2. Anonymous.
3. Dobson, "The Newsletter," Focus on the Family (February 1996).
4. Vern McLellan, *The Complete Book of Practical Proverbs & Wacky Wit* (Wheaton, Illinois: Tyndale House Publishers, Inc., 1996), 182, citing Josh Billings.
5. Donald Grey Barnhouse, *Bible Truth Illustrated* (Grand Rapids: Fleming H. Revell, 1979), 252.
6. Paul E. Hovey, *The Treasury for Special Days & Occasions* (Grand Rapids: Fleming H. Revell, 1989), 124, citing Theodore Roosevelt.
7. Statistics courtesy of Sports World Ministries.
8. Elon Foster, *6000 Classic Sermon Illustrations* (Grand Rapids: Baker Books, 1993), 460.
9. Benjamin R. De Jong, *The Speaker's Quotebook* (Grand Rapids: Baker Books, 1976), 199.
10. David F. Burgess, *Encyclopedia of Sermon Illustrations* (St. Louis: Concordia Publishing House, 1988), 152, excerpted from *The Concordia Pulpit*, 1930-1985, © Concordia Publishing House.
11. McLellan, 184.
12. *Ibid.*, 165, citing George Washington.
13. *Ibid.*, citing Napoleon Bonaparte.
14. *Ibid.*, 184.
15. Adrian Rogers, used by permission.
16. McLellan, 241.
17. *Ibid.*
18. *Ibid.*, 29.
19. McLellan, 181.

Chapter 2: "Setting the Standard"

1. William J. Federer, *America's God and Country* (Coppell, Texas: FAME Publishing, Inc., 1994), 392.
2. Foster, 460.
3. Barnhouse, *Let Me Illustrate*, 305.

4. *Ibid.*
5. Craig Brian Larson, *Illustrations for Preaching & Teaching; From Leadership Journal* (Grand Rapids: Baker Books, 1993), 126.
6. Foster, 115.
7. Roff Zettersten, *Train Up A Child: Giving Values That Last A Lifetime* (Dallas: Word Publishing, 1991), 49.
8. Larson, 74.
9. De Jong, 68.
10. Foster, 312, citing Sir Joshua Reynolds.
11. De Jong, 204.
12. Burgess, 110.
13. Penelope Leach, "Say What You Mean, Mean What You Say," *Parenting*, April 1989, 56.
14. Hovey, *Treasury for Special Days*, 128, citing Robert C. Dodds in *Two Together*.
15. Larson, 108.

Chapter 3: "Love Never Fails"

1. McLellan, 145.
2. Burgess, 133.
3. Hovey, *Treasury for Special Days*, 137, citing Washington Irving.
4. McLellan, 165.
5. Hovery, *Treasury for Special Days*, 139, citing Victor Hugo.
6. Walter B. Knight, *Knight's Master Book of 4,000 Illustrations* (Grand Rapids: William B. Eerdmans Publishing Company, 1956), 417.
7. Kevin A. Miller, ed. "To Quote," *Leadership* vol. 16, no. 1, citing Jacqueline Kennedy Onassis.
8. De Jong, 199.
9. Foster, 551.
10. Max Lucado, *And the Angels Were Silent* (Portland, Oregon: Multnomah Press, 1992).
11. McLellan, 145, citing Beethoven.
12. Fred Bauer, "The Healing Power of Touch," *Plus: The Magazine of Positive Thinking*, February 1987, 26-28.
13. Burgess, 78.
14. *Ibid.*, 152.
15. Gary Chapman, *The Five Love Languages* (Chicago: Northfield Publishing, 1995).
16. Patrick Morley, *I Surrender* (Brentwood, Tennessee: Wolgemuth & Hyatt, Publishers, Inc., 1990), 278-9.
17. De Jong, 223.
18. Burgess, 131.
19. McLellan, 242.
20. *Ibid.*, 145.

21. McLellan, 44.
22. Foster, 115.
23. Author unknown.

Chapter 4: "Who's the Boss?"

1. Barnhouse, *Let Me Illustrate*, 91.
2. McLellan, 172.
3. *Ibid.*
4. Dobson (February 1996).
5. Burgess, 32.
6. McLellan, 181.
7. Barnhouse, *Let Me Illustrate*, 95-6.
8. Bob Orben, *Quip Trip*, 1985.
9. Hovey, *The Treasury of Inspirational*, 178, citing Mrs. Jonas E. Salk, *Family Circle*.
10. McLellan, 20.
11. Barnhouse, *Let Me Illustrate*, 171.
12. Foster, 610.

Chapter 5: "Can Your Kids Trust You?"

1. Larson, 167.
2. Barnhouse, *Let Me Illustrate*, 231.
3. Knight, 215-6, citing *Tomorrow*.
4. Zettersten, 61.
5. Foster, 333.
6. De Jong, citing D. L. Moody.
7. Burgess, 312, citing Friedrich Nietzshe.
8. Burgess, 128.
9. Larson, 119.
10. Burgess, 172.
11. Larson, 62.
12. Corrie ten Boom, *Corrie ten Boom: Her Story: The Hiding Place, Tramp for the Lord, Jesus is Victor* (New York: Inspirational Press, 1995), 24-5.

Chapter 6: "To Discipline or Not to Discipline? That Isn't a Question!"

1. McLellan, 181.
2. Foster, 347, citing W. Arnot.
3. Hover, *Treasury of Inspirational*, 152, citing Ruth Alexander.
4. McLellan, 44.
5. Jan Marshall, "Still Hanging In There," *Pinnacle*.
6. Robert L. Garner, *Kiwanis Magazine*.

7. Nika Scott, "Discipline Must Be Enforced,"*Tennessean*, September 8, 1983, 90, citing *Universal Press Syndicate*.
8. Hovey, *Treasury for Special Days*, 131, citing Marcelene Cox, *Ladies Home Journal*.
9. Foster, 280.
10. De Jong, 276.
11. *Ibid.*, 130.
12. Hovey, *Treasury of Inspirational*, 66.
13. McLellan, 65, citing Mark Twain.
14. De Jong, 26.
15. *Ibid.*, 130.
16. McLellan, 172.
17. *Ibid.*, 44.

Chapter 7: "Tools for Training: From Rods to Rewards"

1. David Rubin, *The Basics of Effective Discipline* (The Positive Line).
2. De Jong, 130.
3. Burgess, 62, citing Martin Luther.
4. Foster, 66.
5. Charles Jones as cited by Adrian Rogers.
6. James Dobson, "When You Feel Like Calling in the SWAT Team," was adapted from his book *The Strong-Willed Child* © 1978 James Dobson, obtained from America Online Information Service.
7. Leach, 57.
8. Dobson, "SWAT Team."
9. Barnhouse, *Let Me Illustrate*, 91-2.
10. Dobson, "SWAT Team."
11. *Ibid.*, *Treasury of Inspirational*, 152, citing *The Christian Science Monitor*.

Chapter 9: "What Do I Do When . . . ? (Childhood)"

1. Hovey, *Treasury for Special Days*, 125, citing Imogen Fey, *Your Life*.

Chapter 10: "The Heritage of a Holy Home"

1. De Jong, 233, citing Edgar A. Guest.
2. *Ibid.*, 65, citing George Santayana.
3. *Ibid.*, 211, citing William Temple.
4. Burgess, 59.
5. Foster, 459, citing Samuel Goodrich.
6. Morley, 278.
7. Kevin A. Miller, ed. "To Quote," *Leadership* vol. 16, no. 2, citing Samuel Sava.
8. Hovey, *Treasury of Inspirational*, 212, citing Marcelene Cox.
9. *Ibid.*, 249, citing Dorothy Barclay, *The New York Times Magazine*.

Notes

10. McLellan, 181.
11. Morley, 279.
12. Zettersten, ix, citing Tim LaHaye, *You and Your Family*.
13. Hovey, *Treasury for Special Days*, 130, citing Dean William Inge.
14. Federer, 531, citing President Ronald Reagan.
15. Hovey, *Treasury for Special Days*, 125, citing John S. Bonnell, "Power of the Home," *PEO Record*.
16. Terry Williams, "What I Would Have Done Differently," *Parents* (March 1986), 84-87.
17. Bob Benson, *"See You at the House"* (Nashville: Generoux Nelson, 1989), 151-2.